Bass and Drum Synchronicity: The Ultimate Rhythm Section Workout

by Jason Prushko and Corey Dozier

Audio Contents

1 Rhythm 1	14 Rhythm 14	27 Rhythm 27	40 Rhythm 40
2 Rhythm 2	15 Rhythm 15	28 Rhythm 28	41 Rhythm 41
3 Rhythm 3	16 Rhythm 16	29 Rhythm 29	42 Rhythm 42
4 Rhythm 4	17 Rhythm 17	30 Rhythm 30	43 Rhythm 43
5 Rhythm 5	18 Rhythm 18	31 Rhythm 31	44 Rhythm 44
6 Rhythm 6	19 Rhythm 19	32 Rhythm 32	45 Rhythm 45
7 Rhythm 7	20 Rhythm 20	33 Rhythm 33	46 Rhythm 46
8 Rhythm 8	21 Rhythm 21	34 Rhythm 34	47 Rhythm 47
9 Rhythm 9	22 Rhythm 22	35 Rhythm 35	48 Rhythm 48
10 Rhythm 10	23 Rhythm 23	36 Rhythm 36	49 Rhythm 49
11 Rhythm 11	24 Rhythm 24	37 Rhythm 37	50 Rhythm 50
12 Rhythm 12	25 Rhythm 25	38 Rhythm 38	
13 Rhythm 13	26 Rhythm 26	39 Rhythm 39	

© 2013 BY MEL BAY PUBLICATIONS, INC., PACIFIC, MO 63069.
ALL RIGHTS RESERVED. INTERNATIONAL COPYRIGHT SECURED. B.M.I. MADE AND PRINTED IN U.S.A.
No part of this publication may be reproduced in whole or in part, or stored in a retrieval system, or transmitted in any form
or by any means, electronic, mechanical, photocopy, recording, or otherwise, without written permission of the publisher.

Visit us on the Web at www.melbay.com — E-mail us at email@melbay.com

Table of Contents

Introduction..2	Rhythm 26..39
Rhythm 1...3	Rhythm 27..40
Rhythm 2...4	Rhythm 28..41
Rhythm 3...5	Rhythm 29..42
Rhythm 4...6	Rhythm 30..43
Rhythm 5...7	Rhythm 31..44
Rhythm 6...8	Rhythm 32..45
Rhythm 7...9	Rhythm 33..46
Rhythm 8...10	Rhythm 34..47
Rhythm 9...10	Rhythm 35..47
Rhythm 10...11	Rhythm 36..48
Rhythm 11...12	Rhythm 37..50
Rhythm 12...12	Rhythm 38..51
Rhythm 13...13	Rhythm 39..52
Rhythm 14...14	Rhythm 40..53
Rhythm 15...16	Rhythm 41..54
Rhythm 16...18	Rhythm 42..56
Rhythm 17...20	Rhythm 43..58
Rhythm 18...22	Rhythm 44..60
Rhythm 19...23	Rhythm 45..61
Rhythm 20...24	Rhythm 46..63
Rhythm 21...27	Rhythm 47..67
Rhythm 22...30	Rhythm 48..70
Rhythm 23...34	Rhythm 49..72
Rhythm 24...35	Rhythm 50..74
Rhythm 25...36	About the Authors..................................75-76

Introduction

This book is meant to challenge you in every way. With that said, we will break down playing in different styles such as rock, hip-hop, latin and blues along with adding odd-time signatures and difficult melodic lines for the bassist. The book starts at a medium skill-level and gets increasingly more challenging as it goes on. There is a CD and an audio sample for each example with a suggested tempo. Feel free to play at any tempo once you have mastered the examples as well as expand upon them as well. This should be a fun way to get better with your fellow bassist or drummer and a great way to expand your pocket when holding down a groove. Some true inspirations for these examples and great artists you can check out that capture a lot of what's done in this book are: Return to Forever, Between the Buried and Me, Dream Theater, Hi-Tek, Charles Mingus, Mean Little Blanket, Dillinger Escape Plan, Tito Puente, Lettuce, The Roots.

Rhythm 1

This example is meant to put you in a real life situation playing rock music. The point is to hold down a steady groove at a medium-fast tempo locking in rhythmically with the occasional bass guitar fill. Being able to play a steady repeating riff while not varying far off it is very important in a song context.

Rhythm 2

Again, this example is focused on locking up rhythmically but this time in a hip hop setting. Also adding drum fills to the mix as well showing how switching off and making small fills through a riff can spice up any groove.

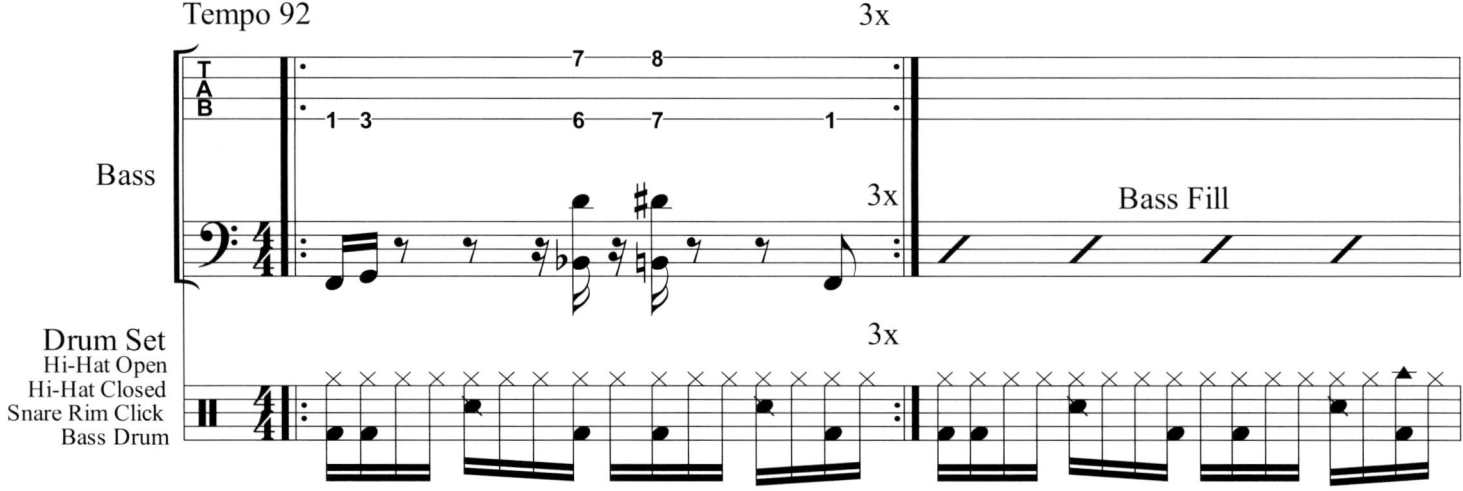

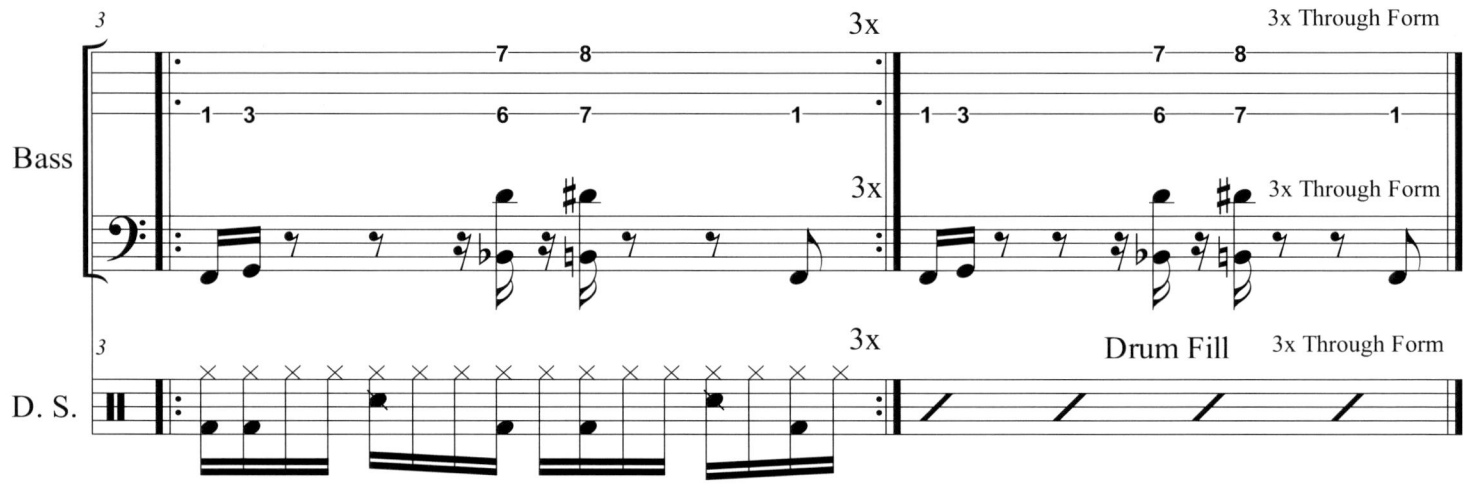

4

Rhythm 3

Example 3 is all about playing in 5/8 with a rock style. The Bass Guitar holds down a steady riff while the drums color it in with a few different beats adding fills to paint the rhythmic style of the bassist.

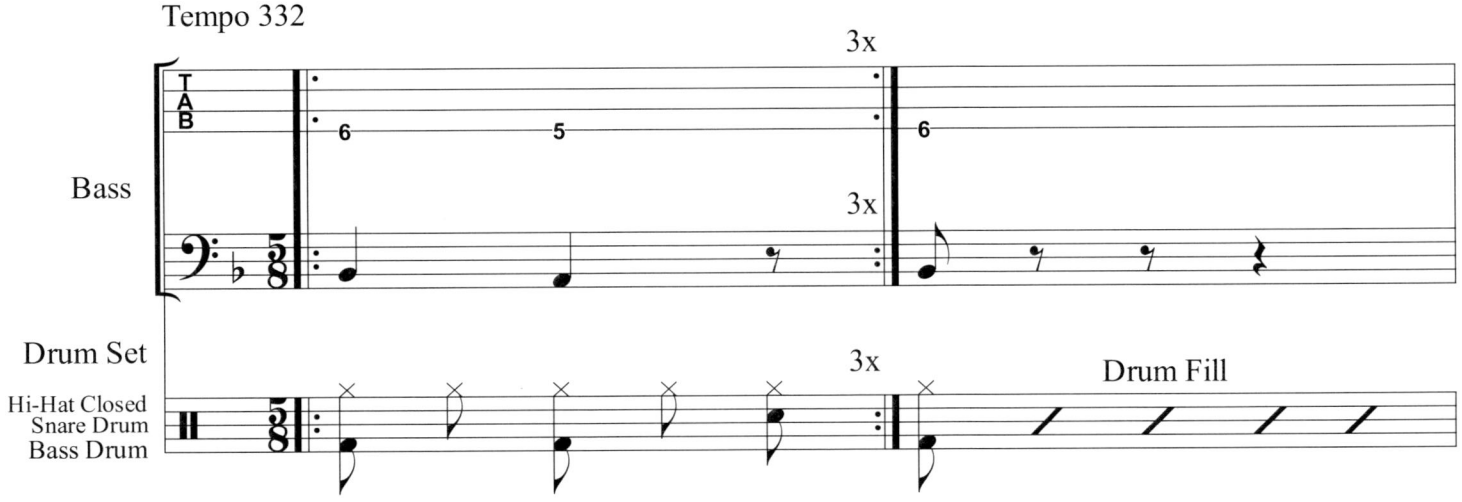

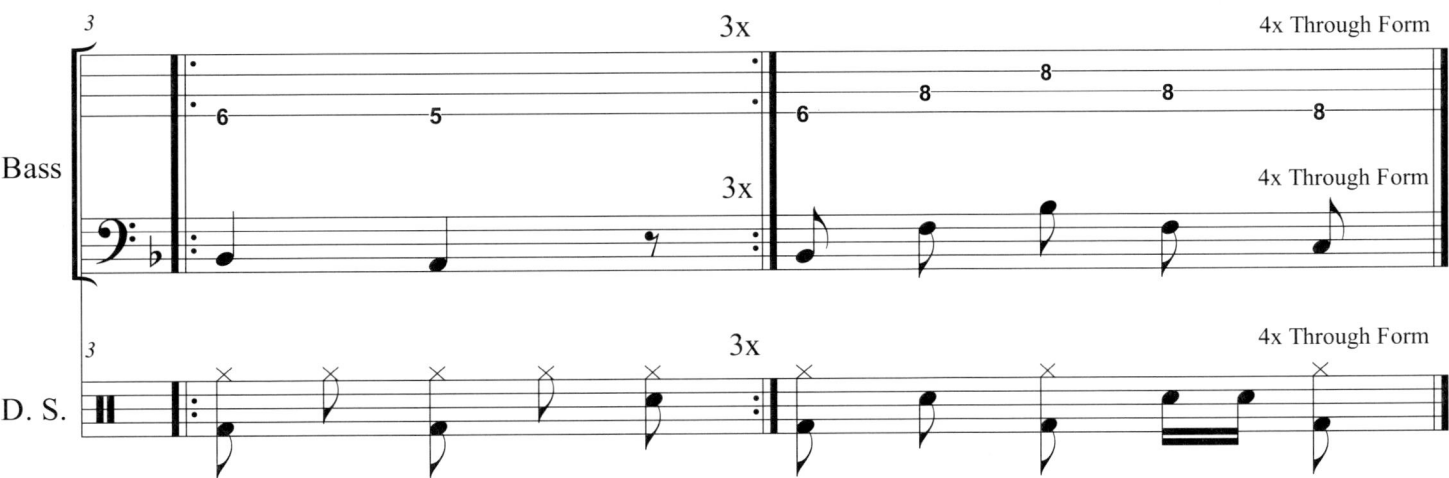

Track 4

Rhythm 4

This next example is all about playing in 5/4. Designed to be as if you were playing a modern rock song with a little twist added to it. The form being in A and B sections, while the drummer fills up each new section.

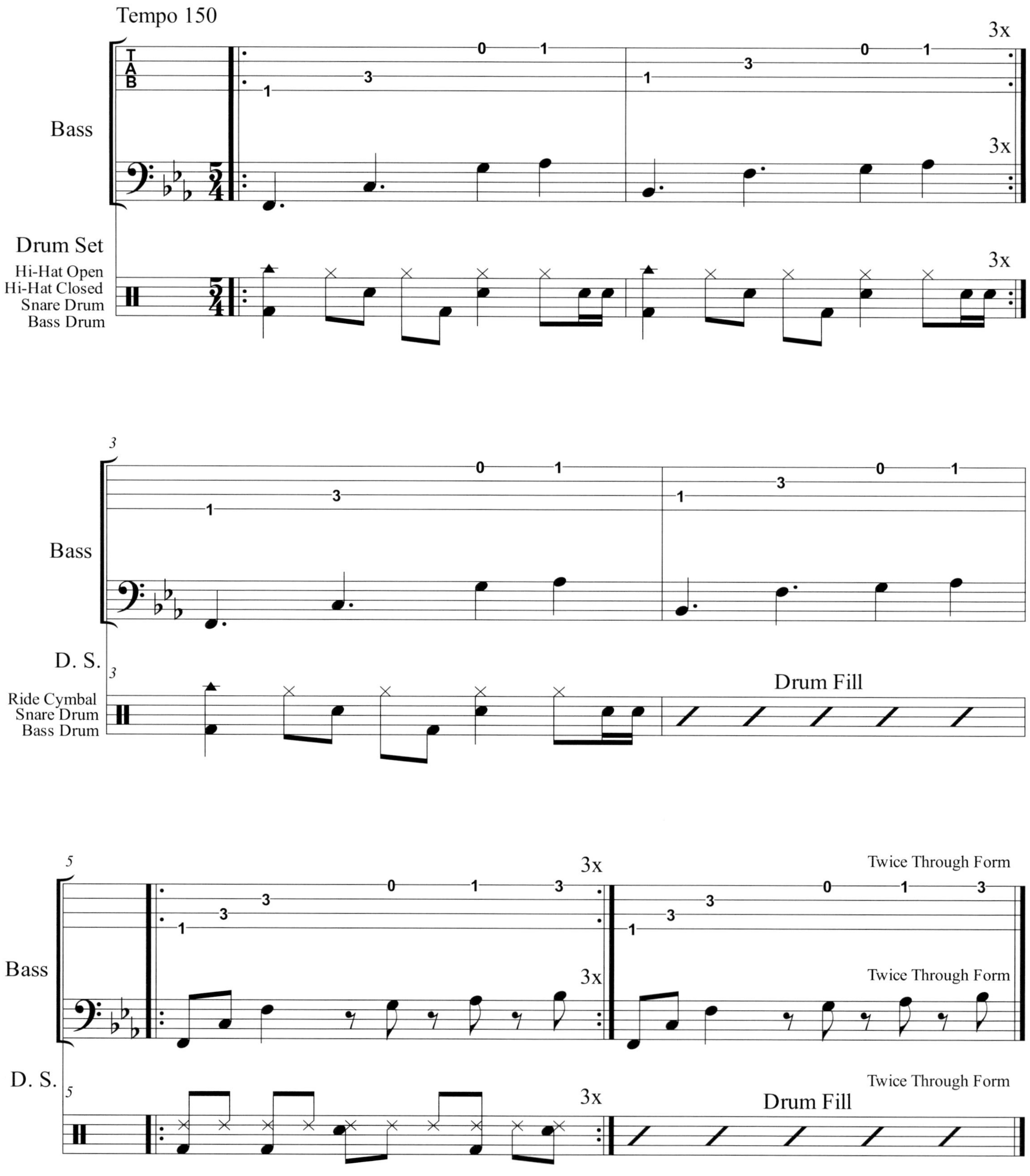

Track 5

Rhythm 5

Example 5 focuses on playing in 5/8 but in the style of funk/hip hop. Instead of filling through it or playing busy lines, this example shows how you can just groove in 5/8 and change it up by putting different emphasis on different beats.

Tempo 260

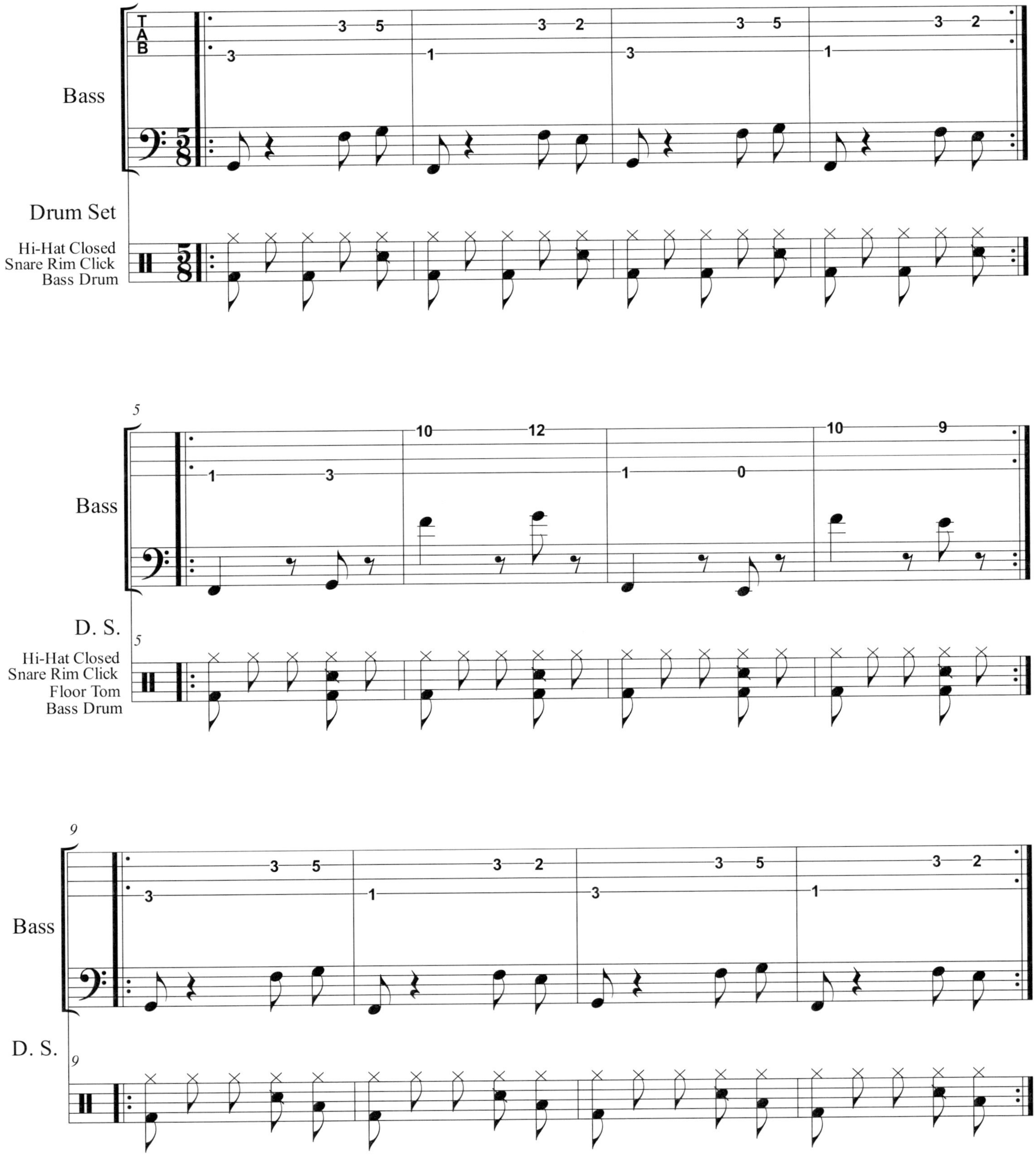

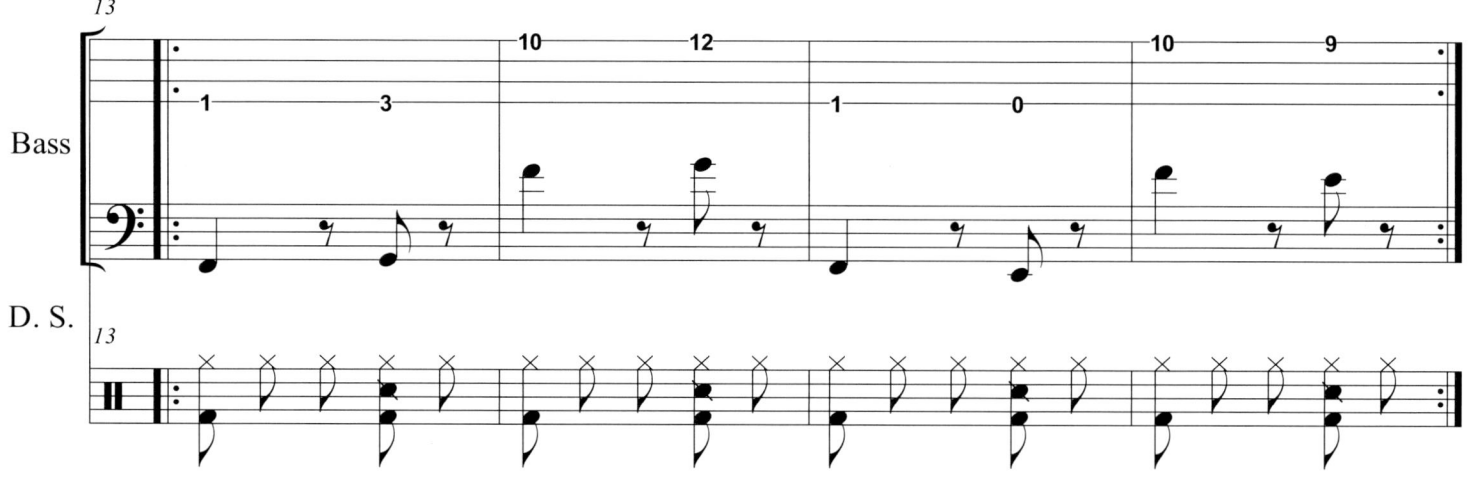

🔊 Rhythm 6
Track 6

This next example is about playing in 5/4. What makes this different than 5/8 is being able to to use quarter notes along with 8th and 16th notes, typically at a slower to medium tempo so you can really feel each beat.

Rhythm 7

This next one is playing 7/8 in a fast rock style. It's all about the drummer painting the bass line in different ways, so there's two different ways shown with drum fills leading to each section.

Rhythm 8

Example 8 shows you how to play a dotted quarter note feel in 7/4. This works great in a rock/hard rock setting. The bassist hinting at triplets while the drummer places a dotted quarter in half time. This switch between quarter note and dotted quarter note can be a cool way to shape a section.

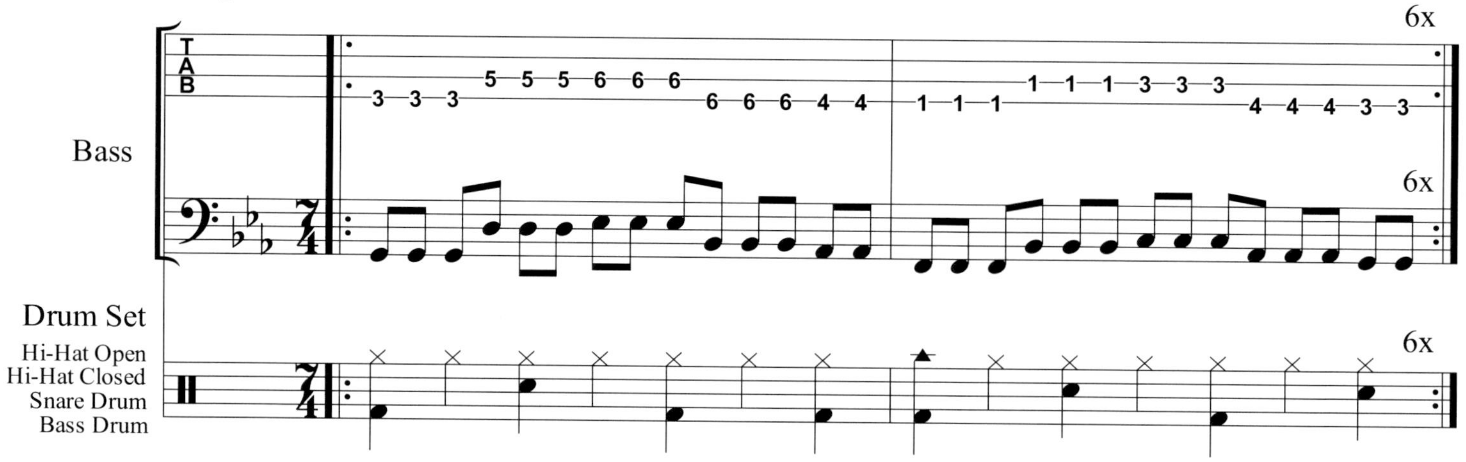

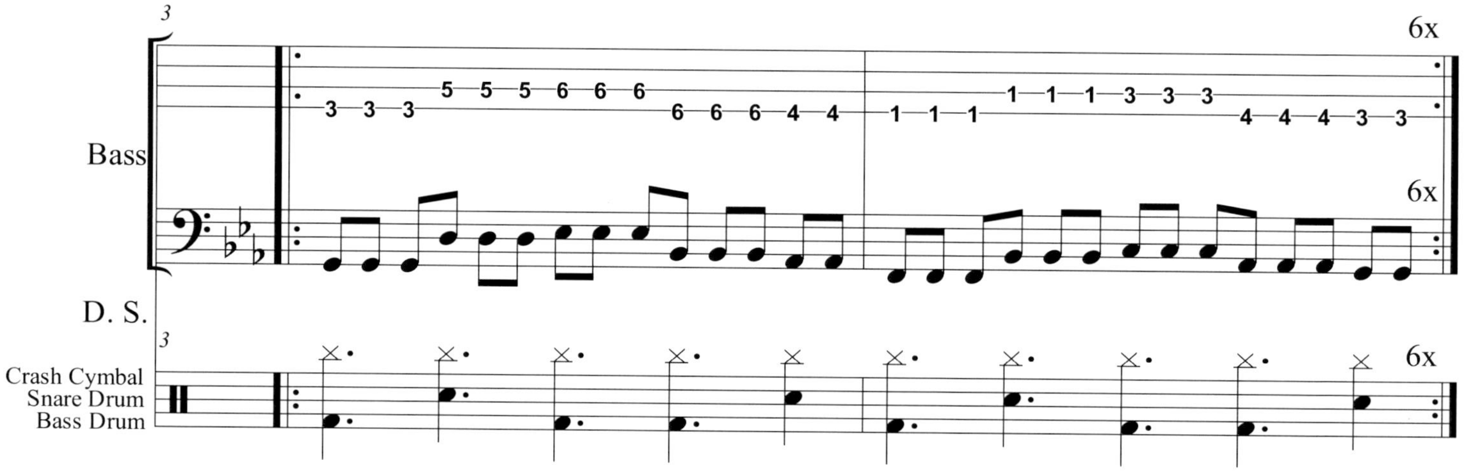

Rhythm 9

This exercise is about playing a steady 2 bar phrase in 7/8 at a quick tempo. Being able to just hold it down is just as important as filling–this example shows that.

Rhythm 10

Example 10 demonstrates playing a real funky groove, but doing so in 7/4. It's really cool and unique to be able to make odd time signatures sound like 4/4. With this example it's all about holding down a funky groove and flowing as if you were in regular 4/4 but with a slight twist added.

Rhythm 11

This exercise is geared at playing 6 over 4. The bassist will be using quarter note triplets in 4/4, while the drummer plays a beat holding down the straight 4/4 feel. This gives the feel of the bass playing 6 over 4.

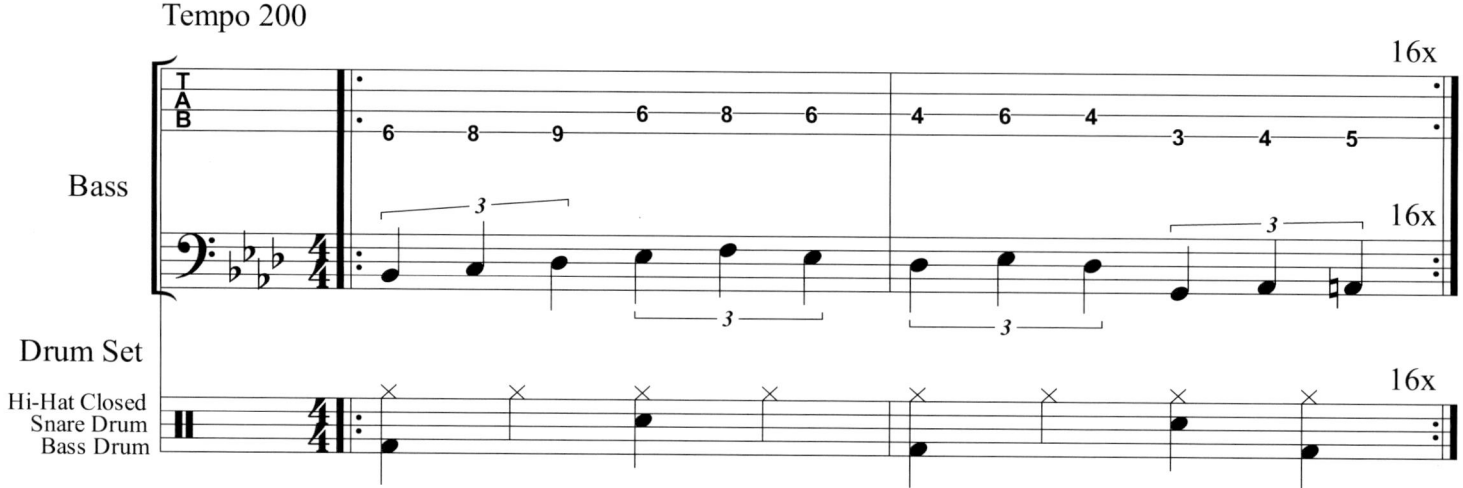

Rhythm 12

Example 12 now switches the bass playing a strict 4/4 groove while the drums focus on playing quarter note triplets in 4/4. The drums now represent playing 6 over 4 in a hip hop setting.

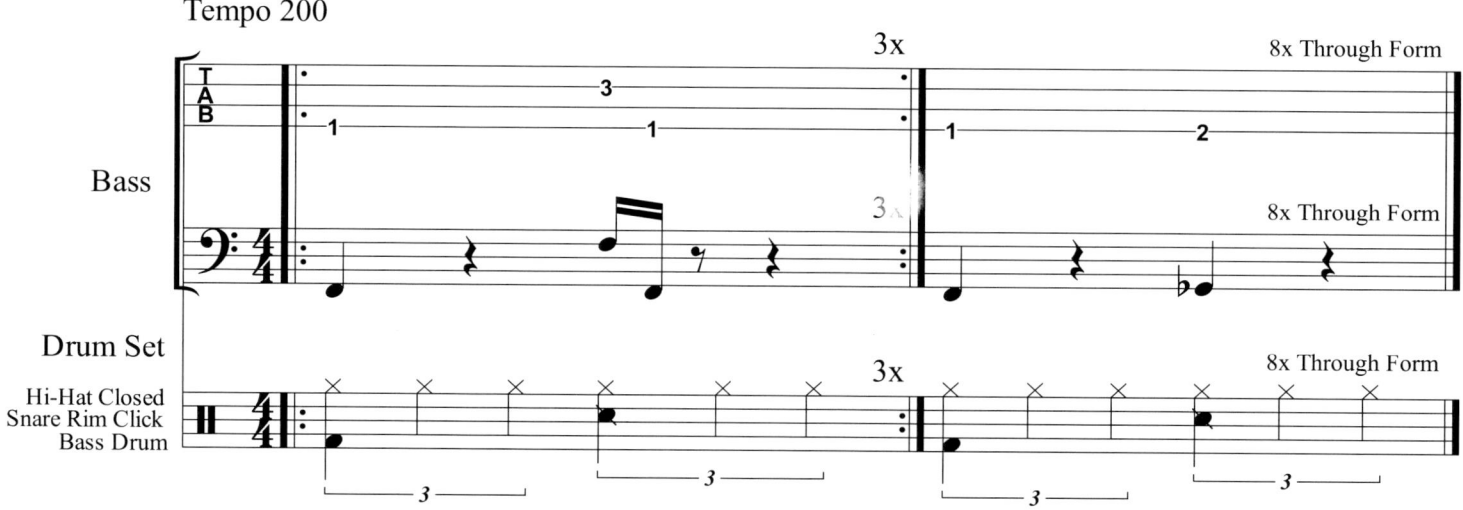

Rhythm 13

This next example continues the 6 over 4 but in more of an interactive way. The drums continue to hold down a crisp steady 4/4 drum beat while the bass implies the 6 over 4 right from the start. Then the bass switches to the 4/4 feel that the drummer was playing previously. This can be what brightens up any funky 4/4 groove.

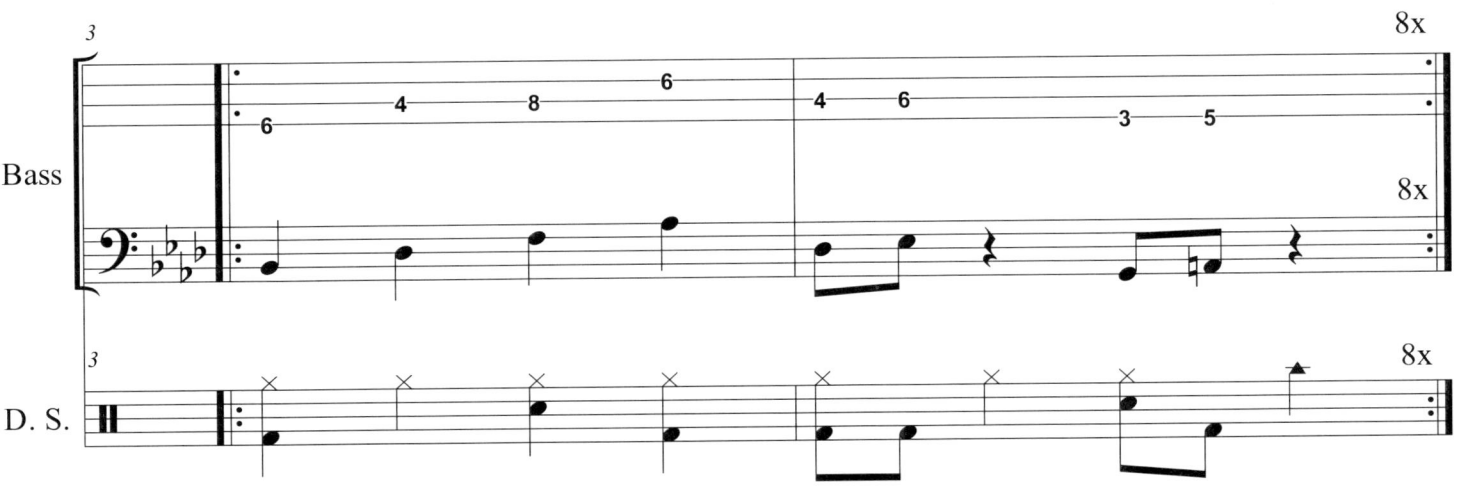

Rhythm 14

This example again focuses on 6 over 4. Since 4/4 is so commonly used, 6 over 4 is such an important tool to have down. This example has the bass playing the 6 throughout and the drums starting in a 4/4 beat, then switching over with the bass–both playing the 6 over 4.

This page has been left blank
to avoid awkward page turns.

Rhythm 15

Example 15 now does the reverse of example 14: the bass holds down a groove in 4/4 while the drums are playing the 6 over 4 right from the start. The drums then will change back to a straight 8th note 4/4 groove matching the bass.

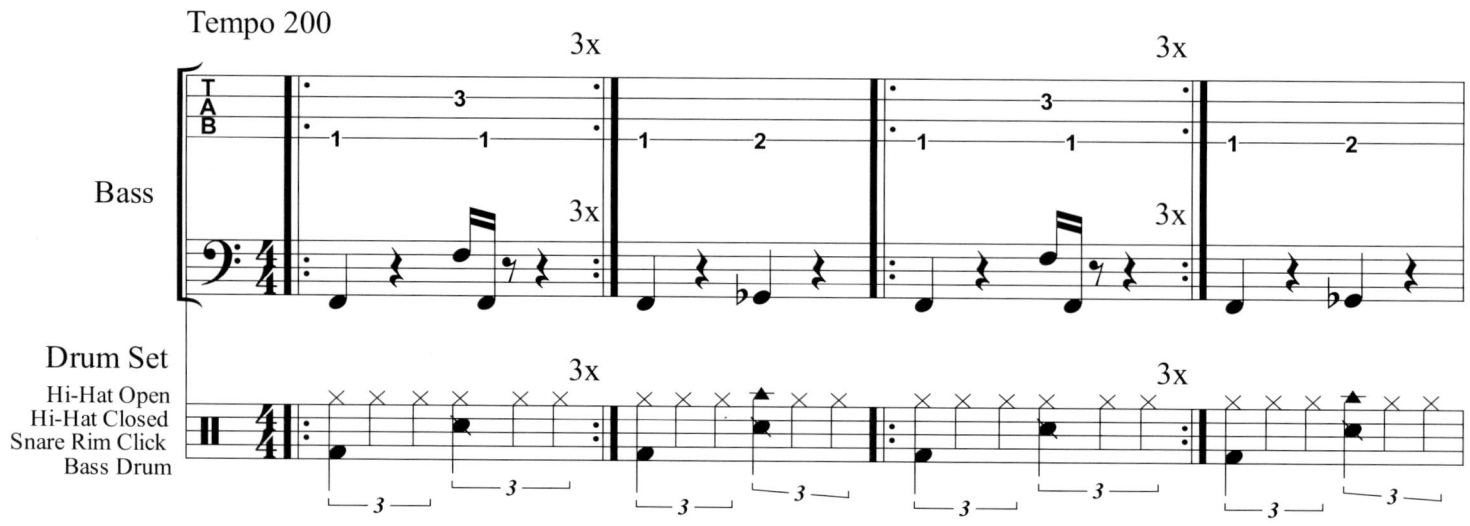
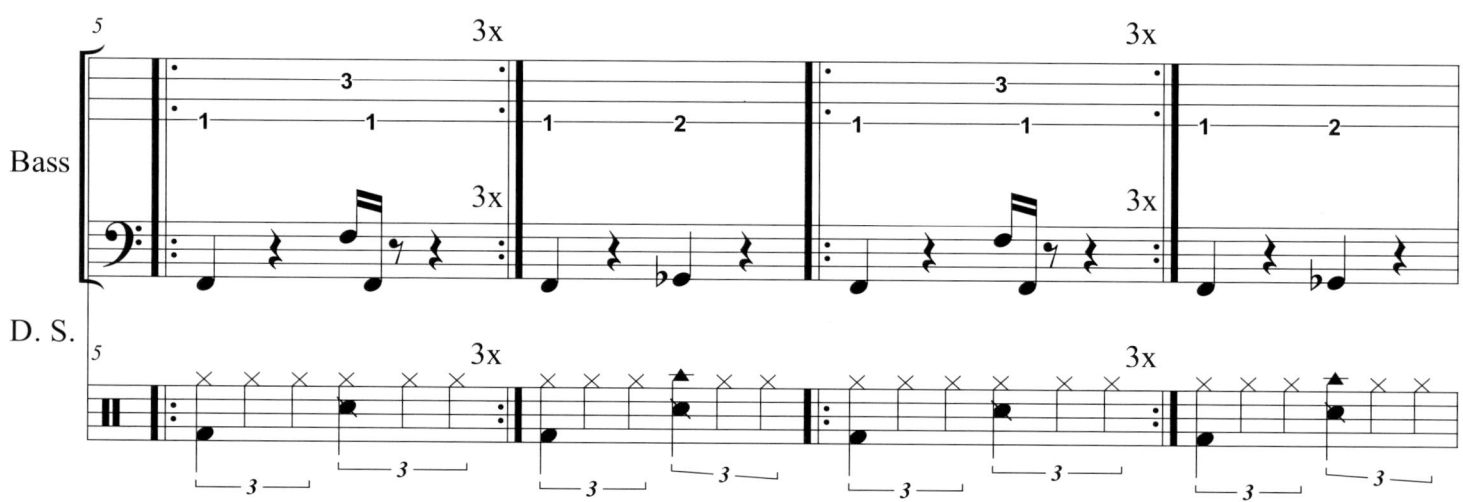
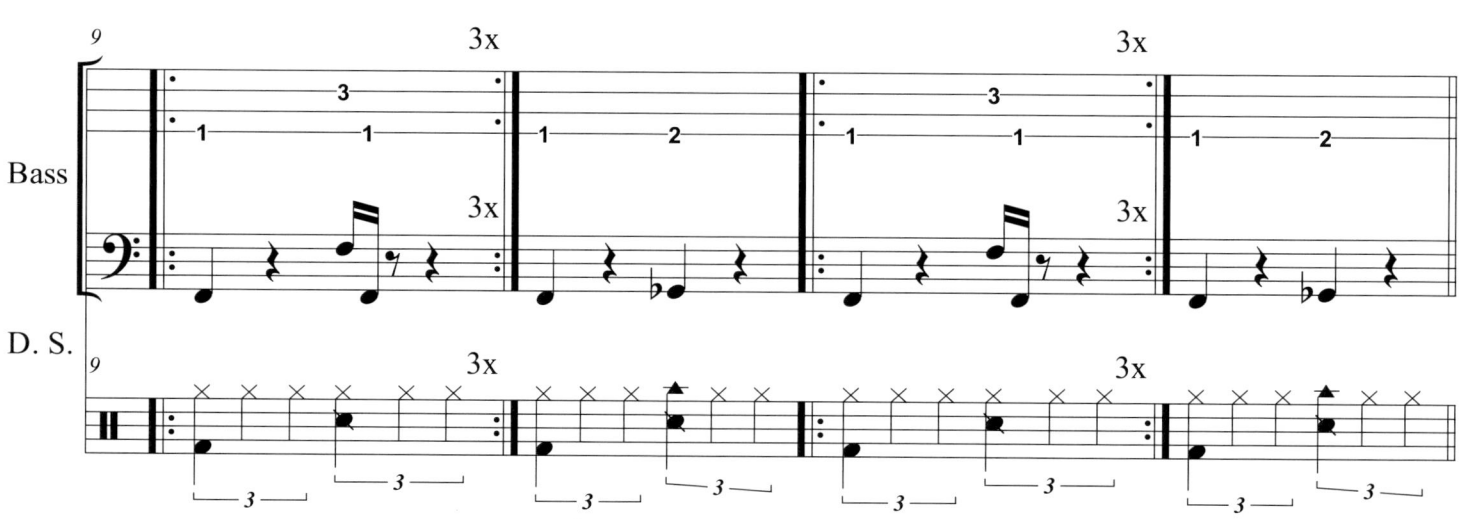

13
Bass
D. S.
3x
17
Bass
D. S.
3x
21
Bass
D. S.
3x

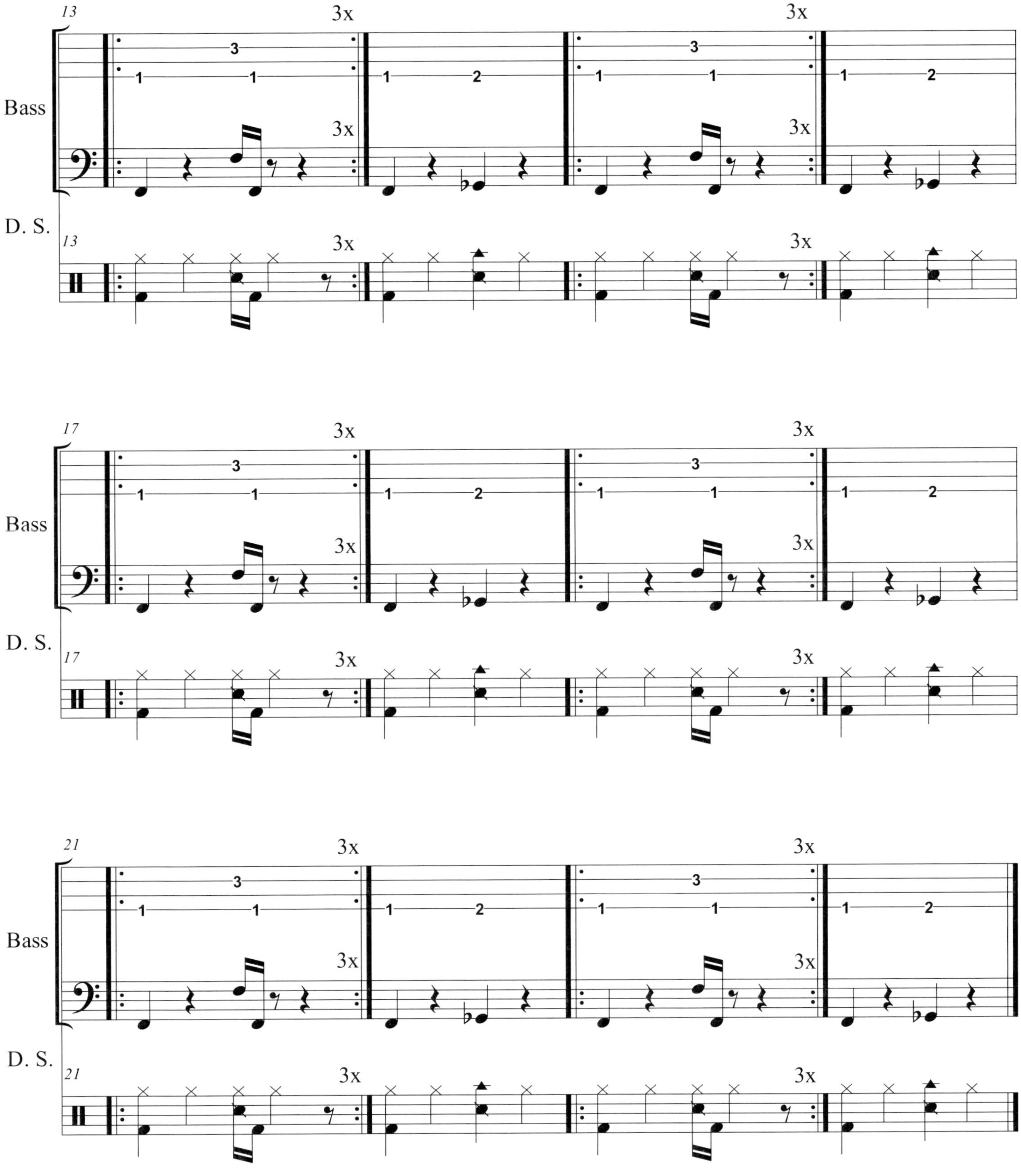

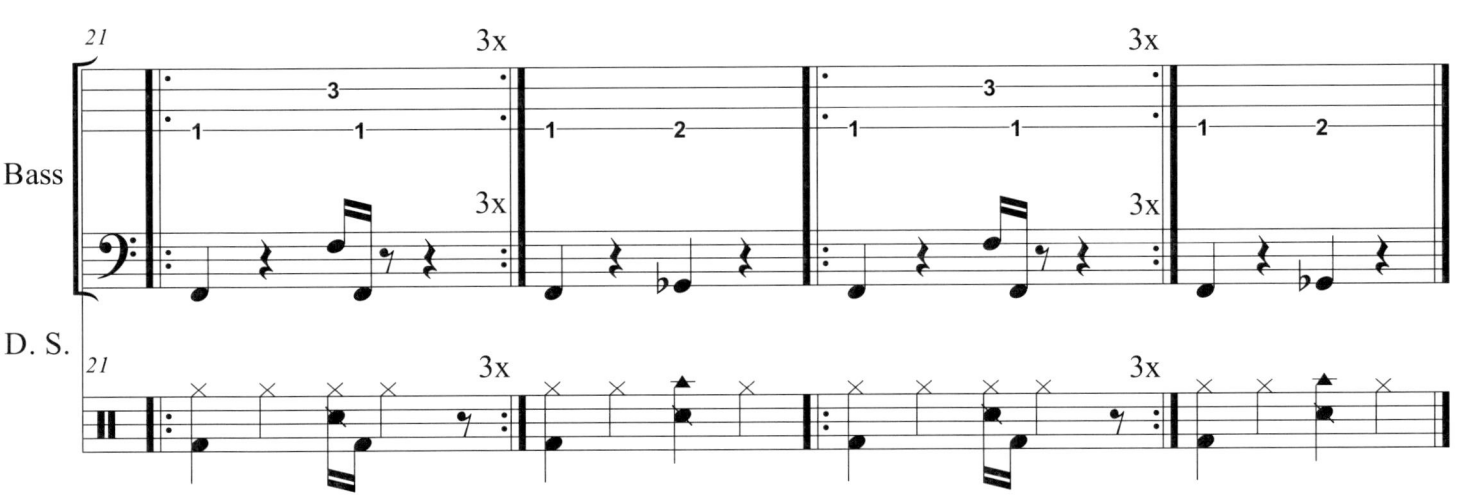

Rhythm 16

This exercise continues the 6 over 4, having the drums play quarter note triplets throughout the whole example, while the bass start with straight 8th notes and 16th notes before switching with the drums to the 6 over 4.

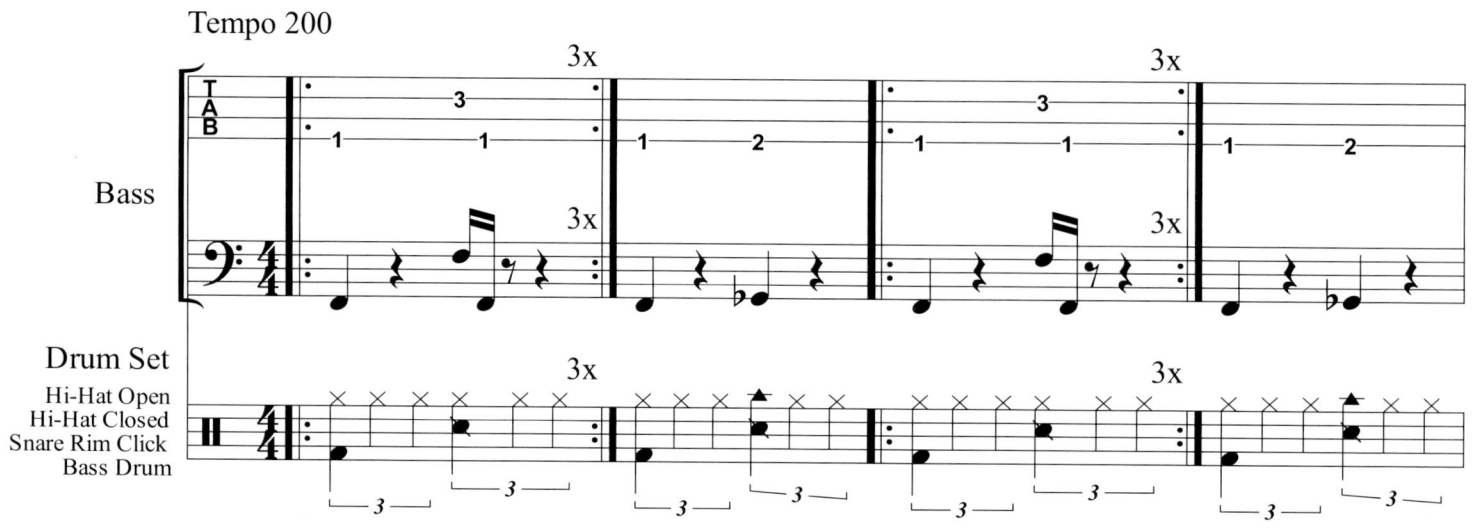

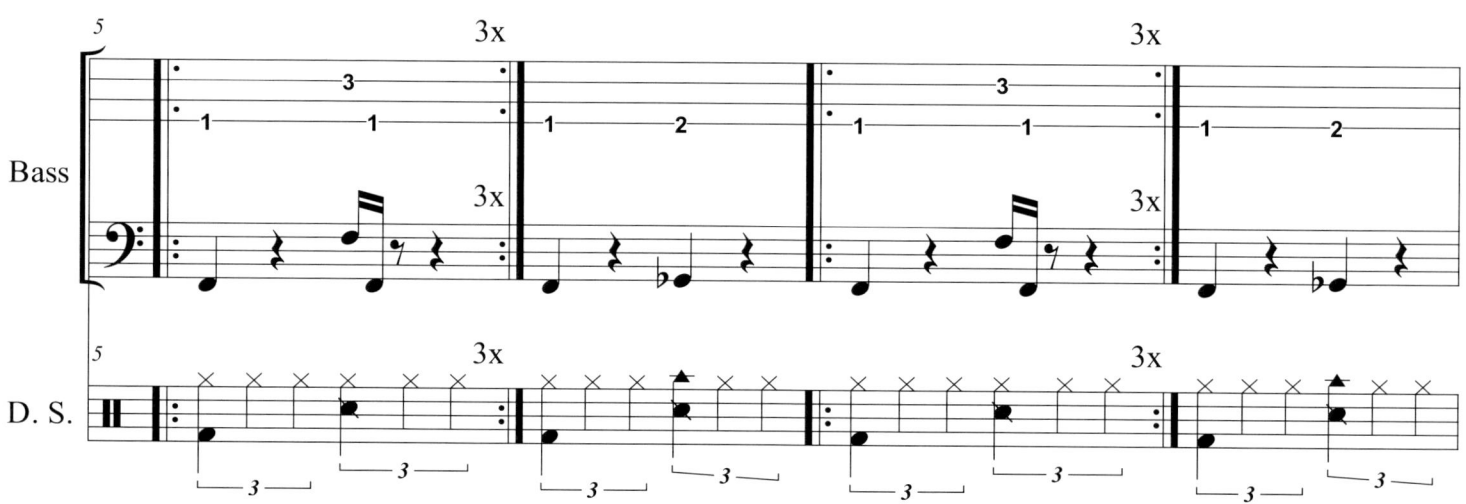

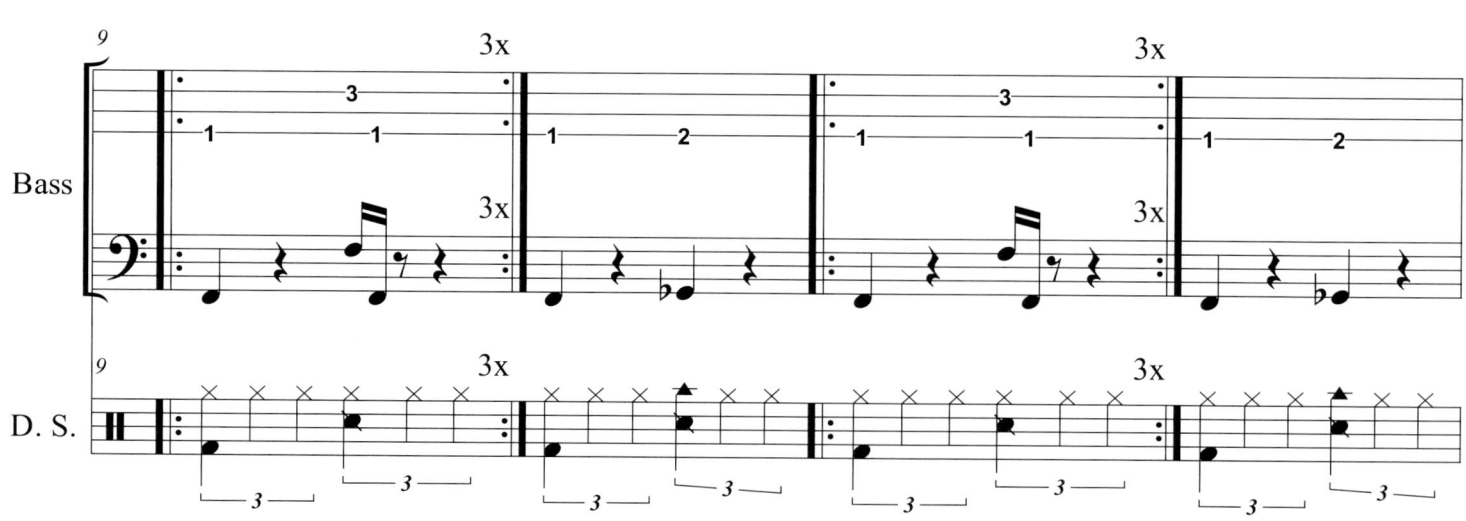

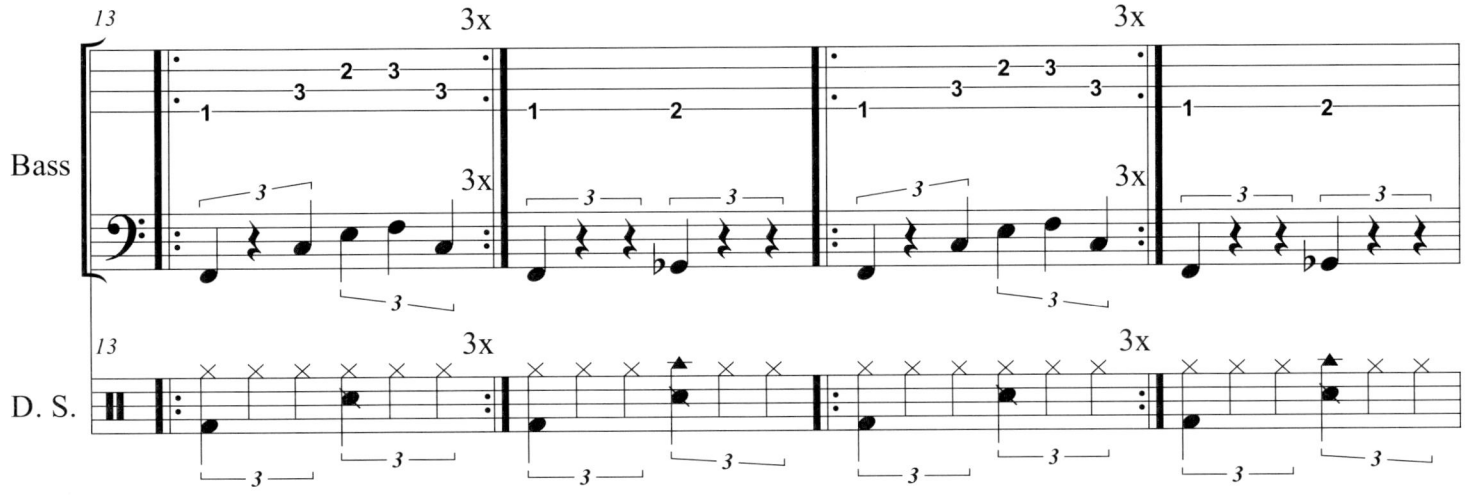
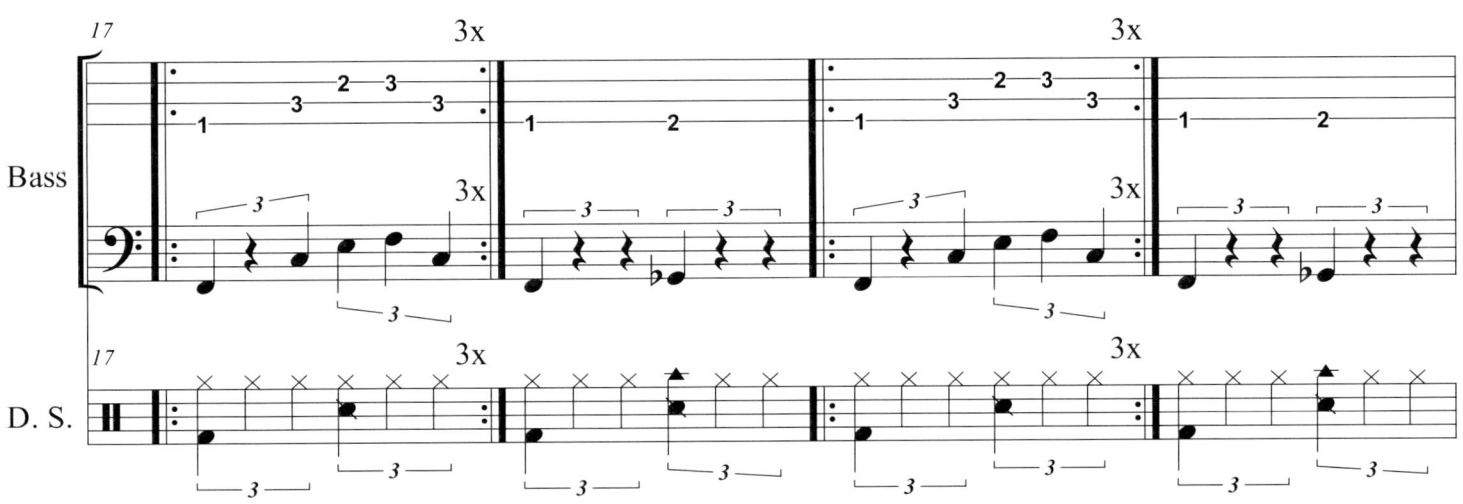
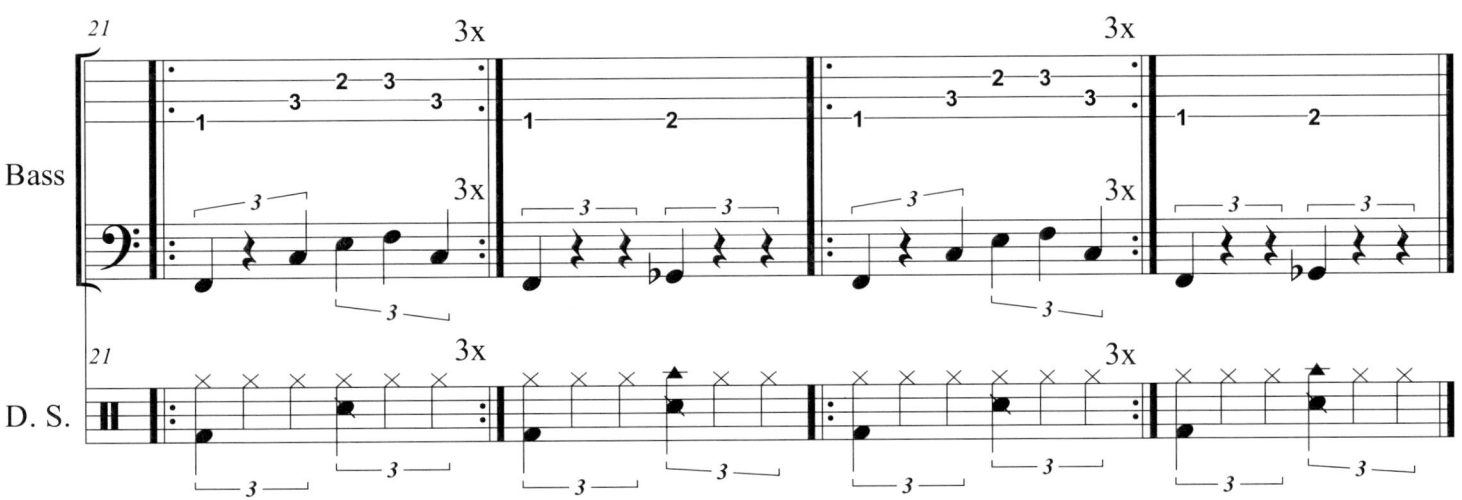

Rhythm 17

Now with all the different 6 over 4 examples prior to this one, this next example throws it at you more randomly: having each instrument switch at different times gives you a taste of what might happen in a real life playing situation.

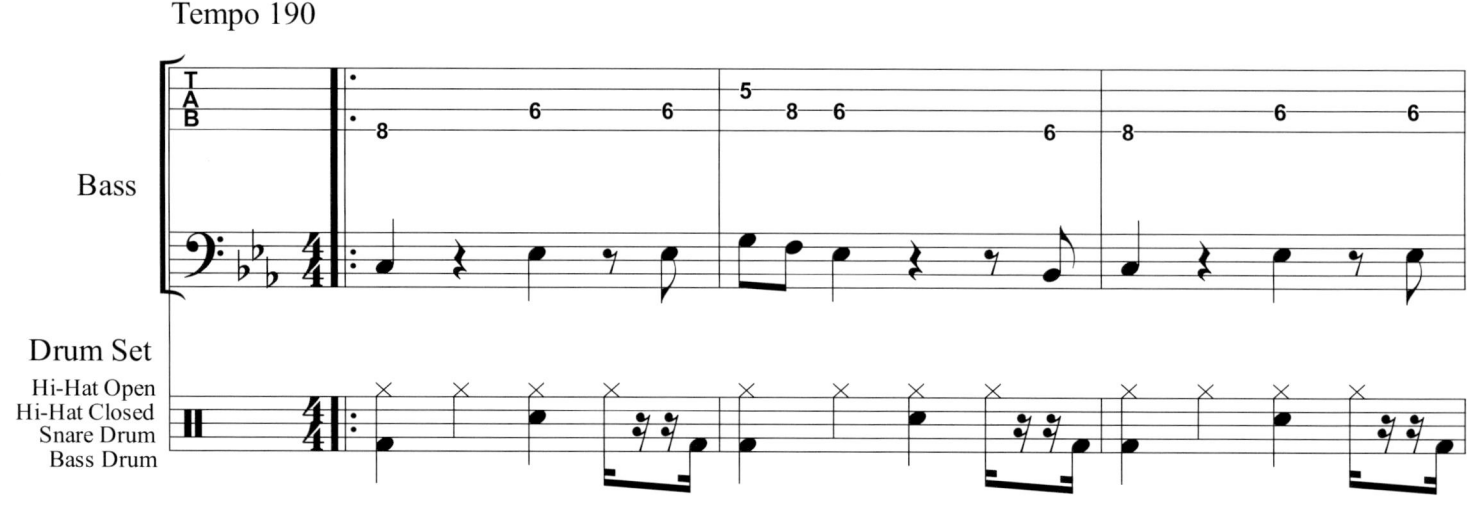
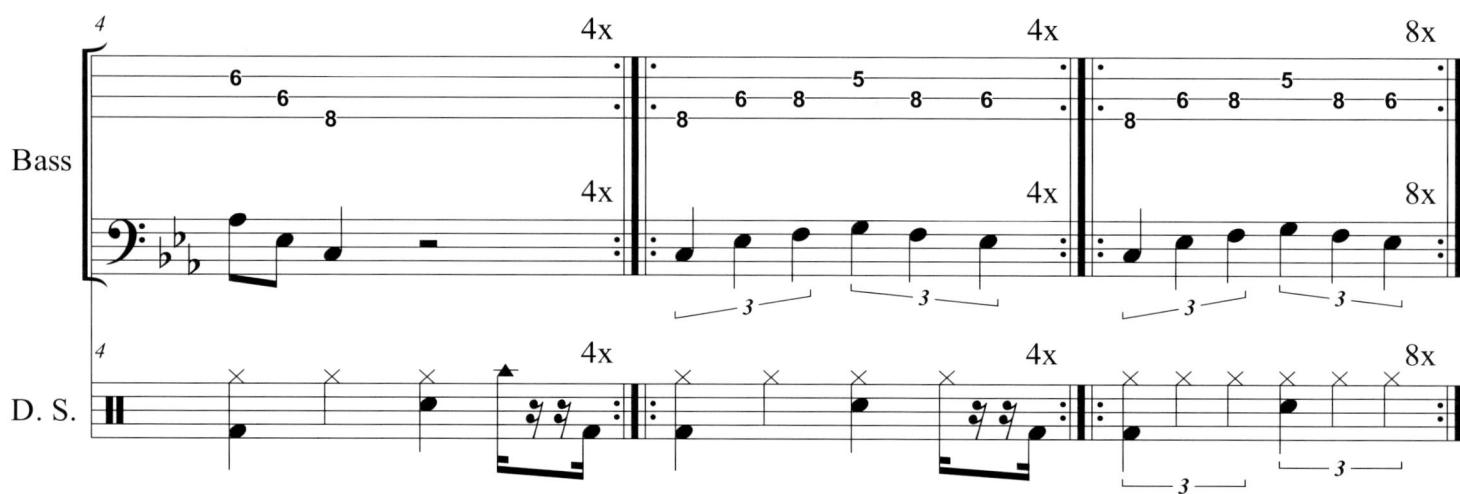
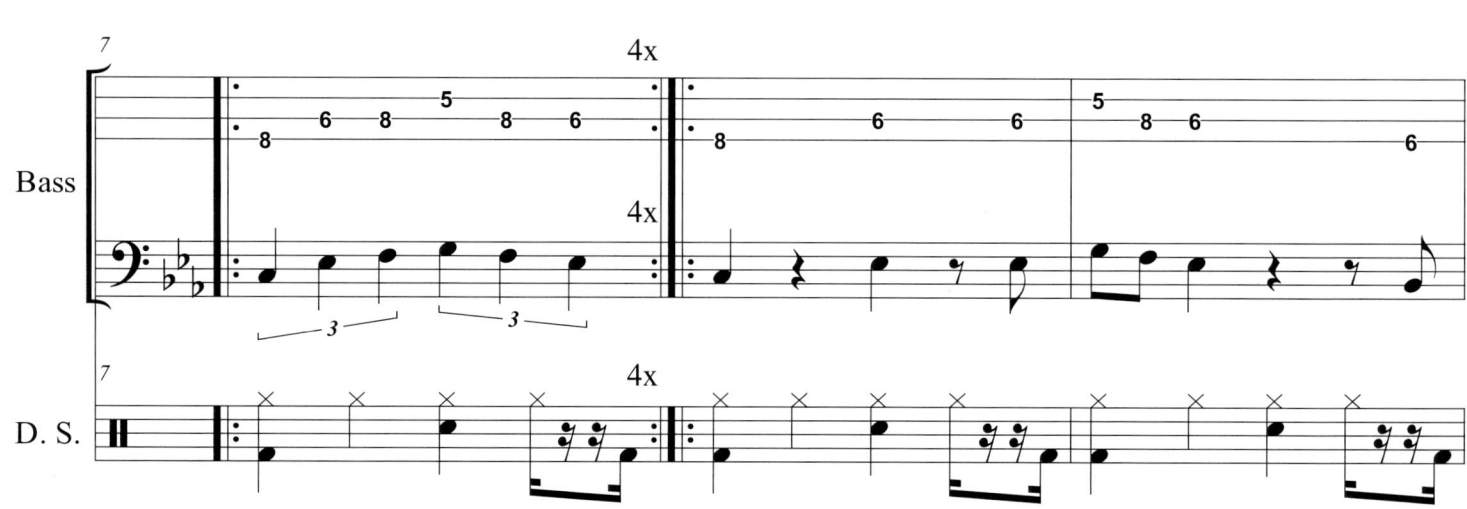

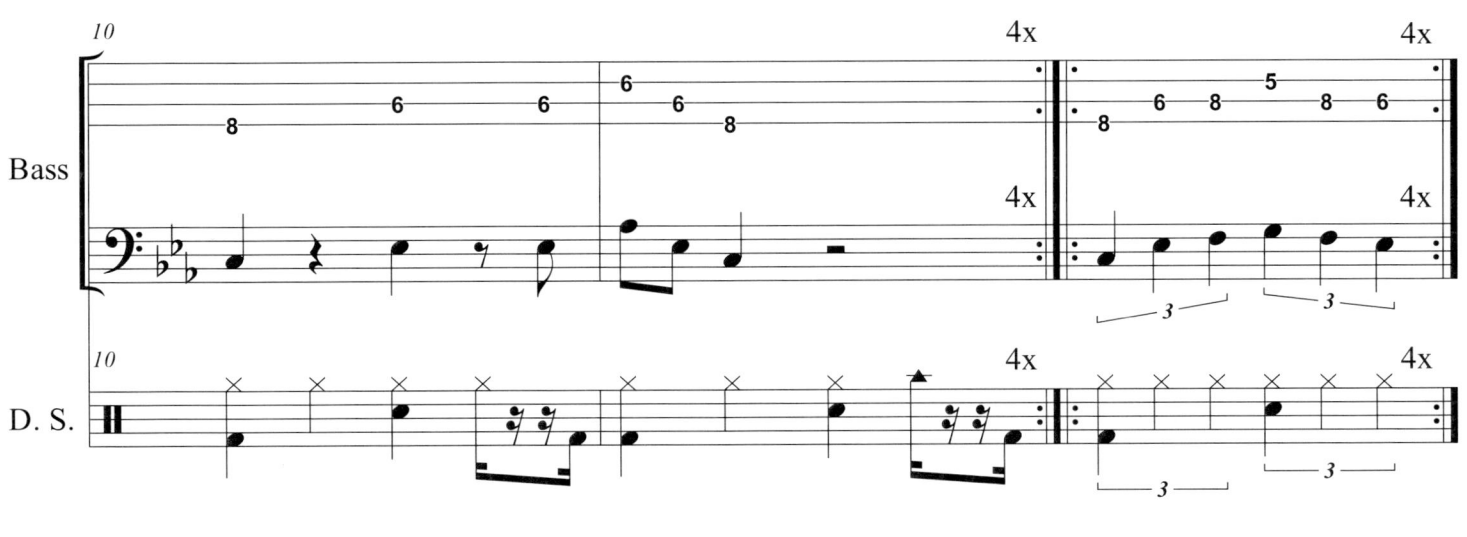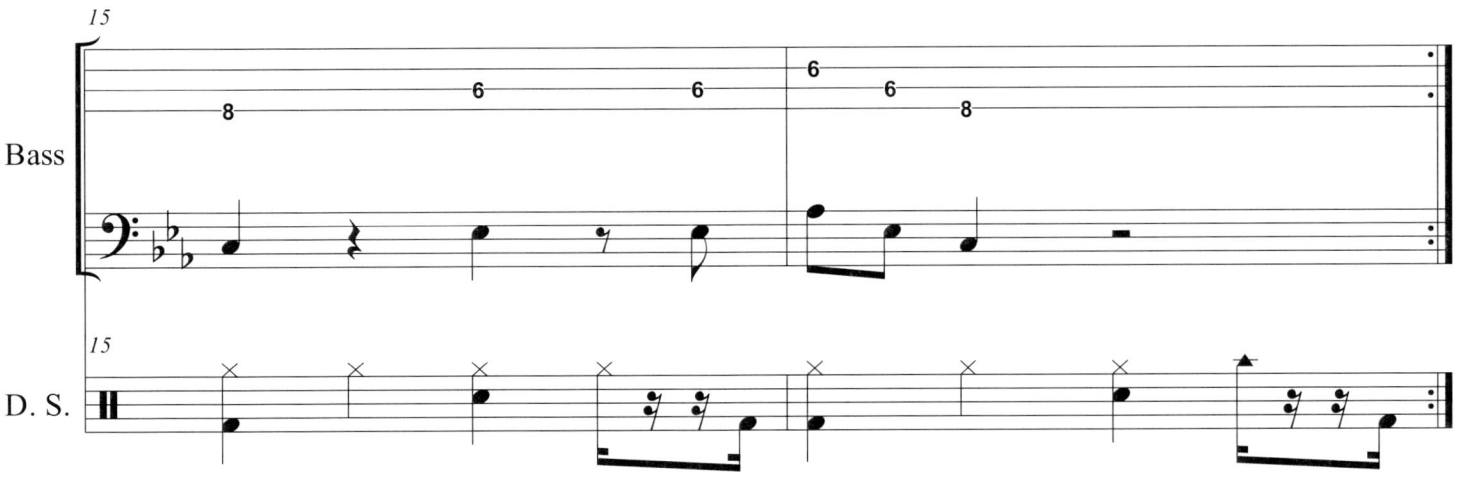

Rhythm 18

Example 18 is a complete mix up of different feels in 4/4. Using 16th notes, 8th notes, quarter notes and triplets to give different types of rhythmic feels in 4/4.

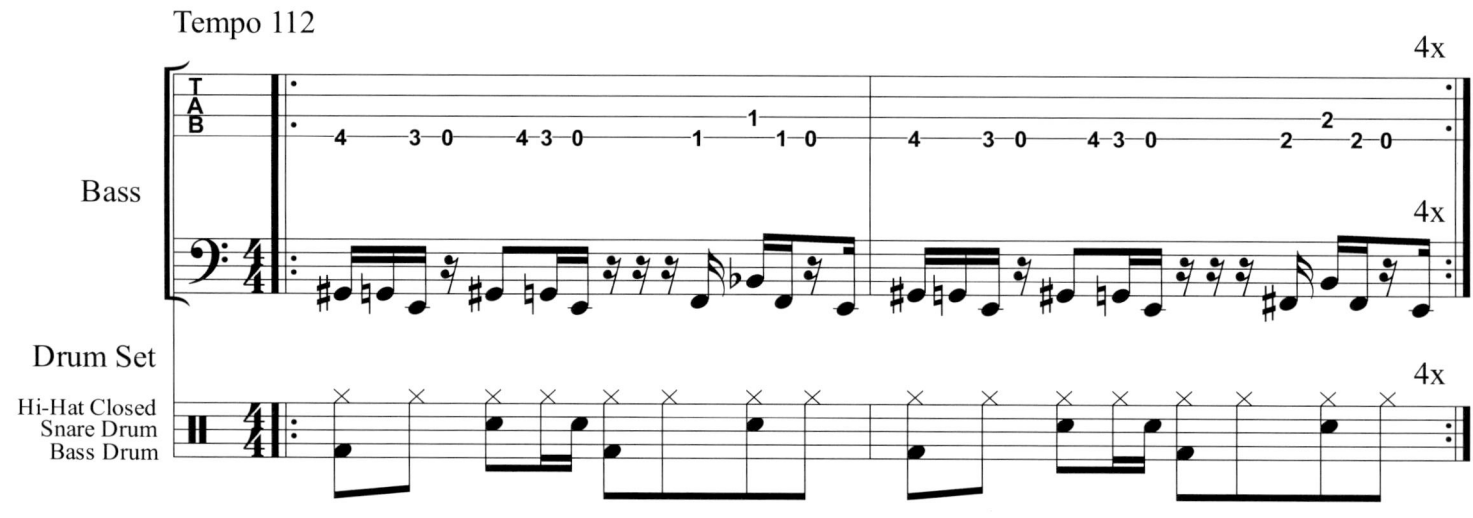

 ## Rhythm 19

This example is focusing on playing in 10/4. It can be really cool to play a funky groove in an odd time but have it sound as if it's in 4/4. This example shows you just that using 10/4 as the odd time.

Rhythm 20

These examples are about switching feels while playing the blues. It's always important to be able to switch and color feels up during choruses in the blues. These next 3 examples show you how to switch from 4/4 to 6/8 and reverse, as well as going from 4/4 to 12/8.

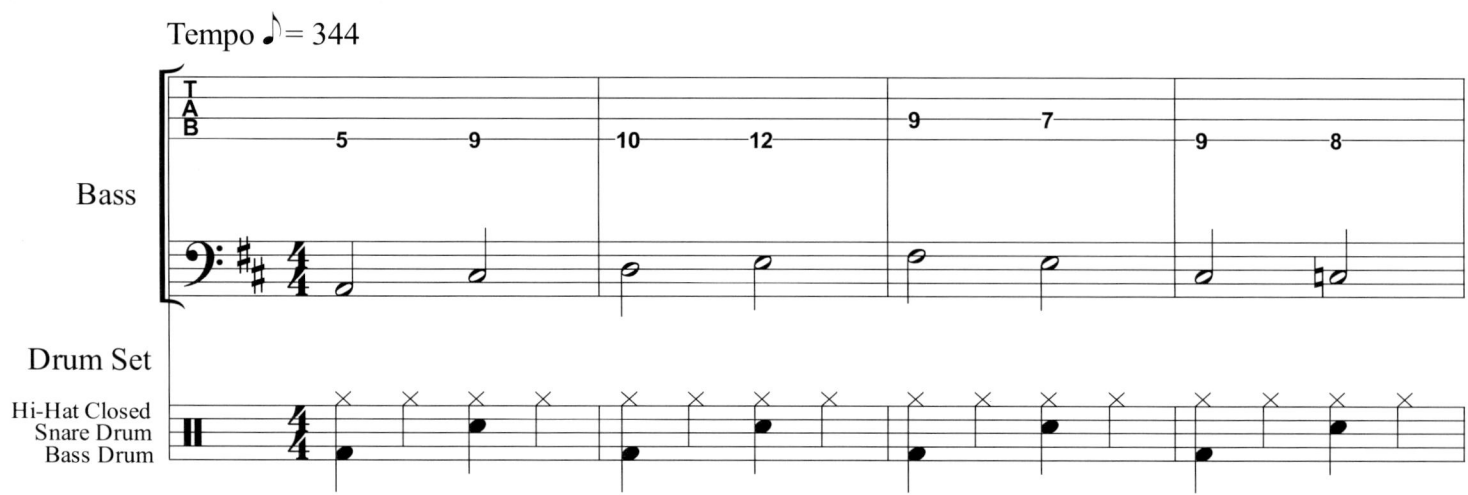

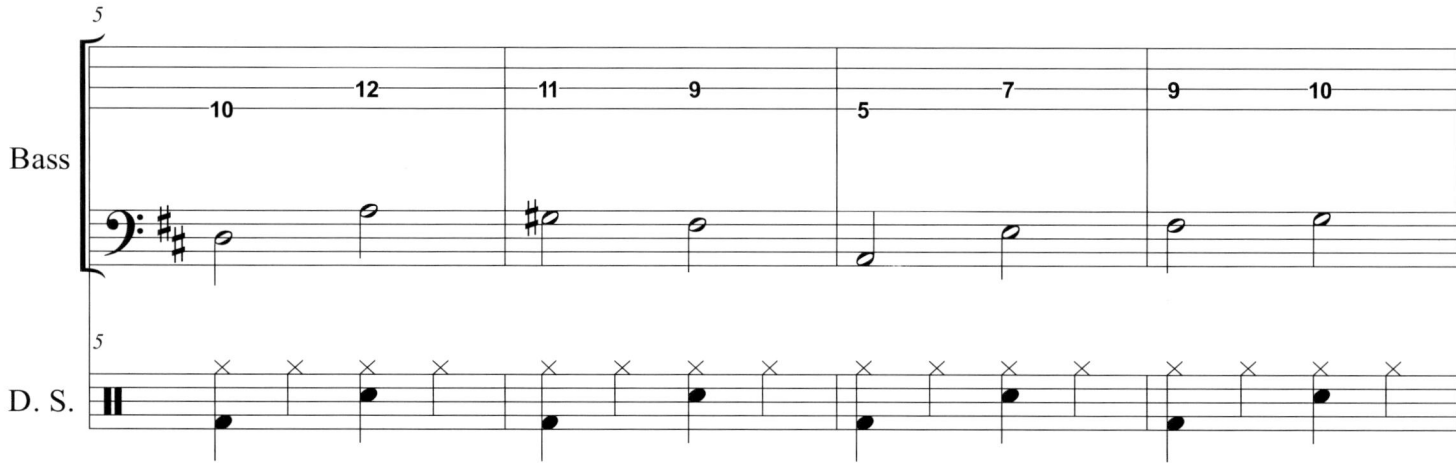

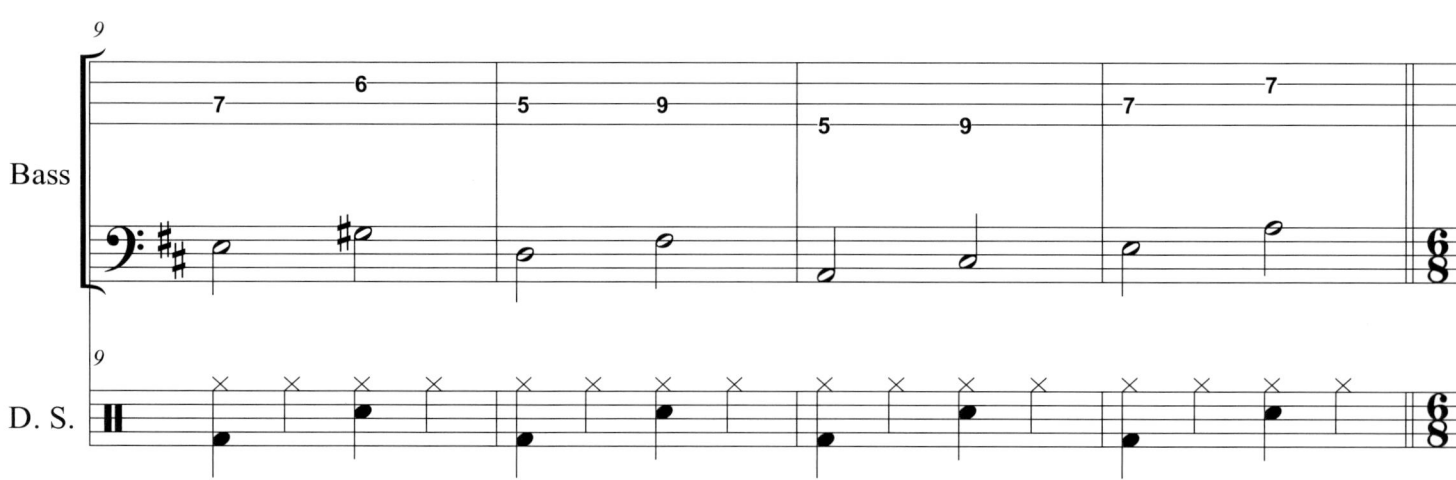

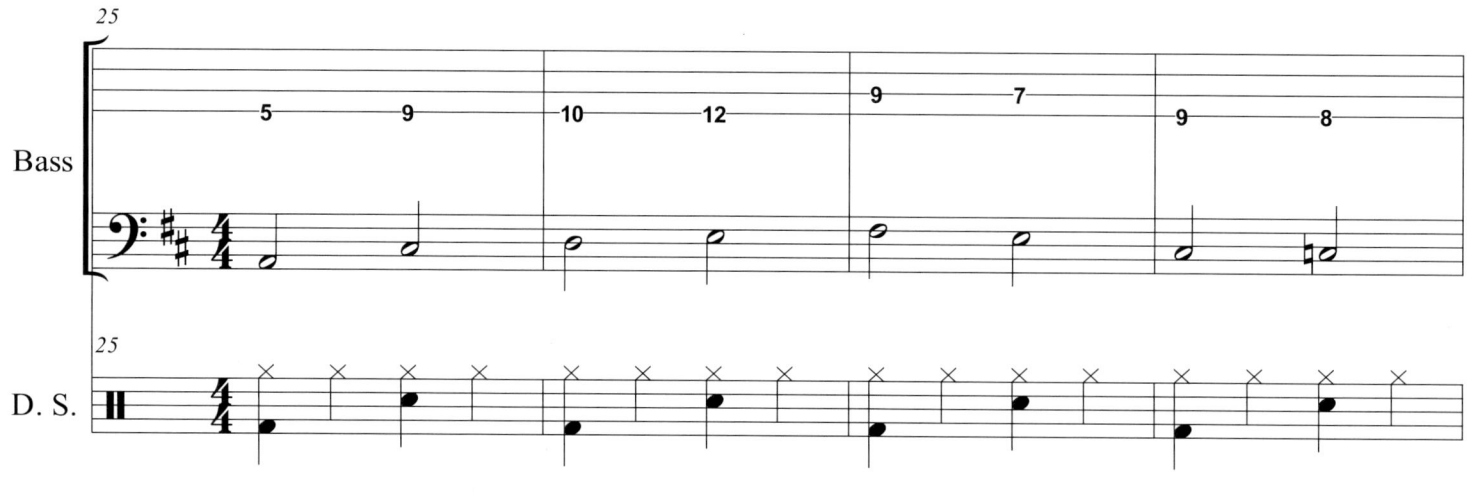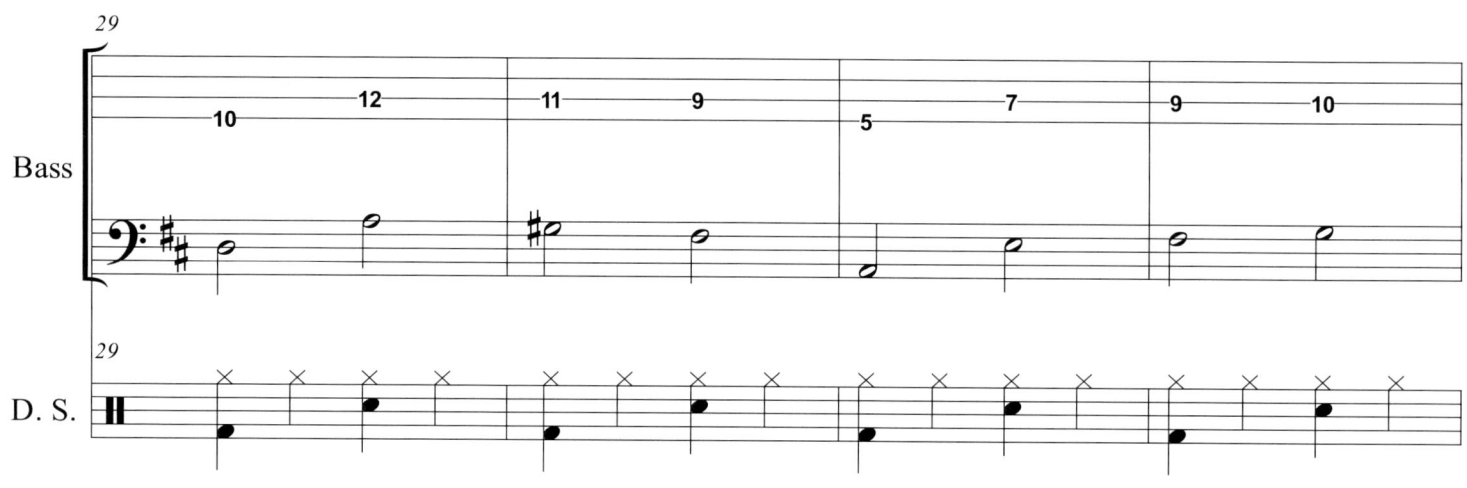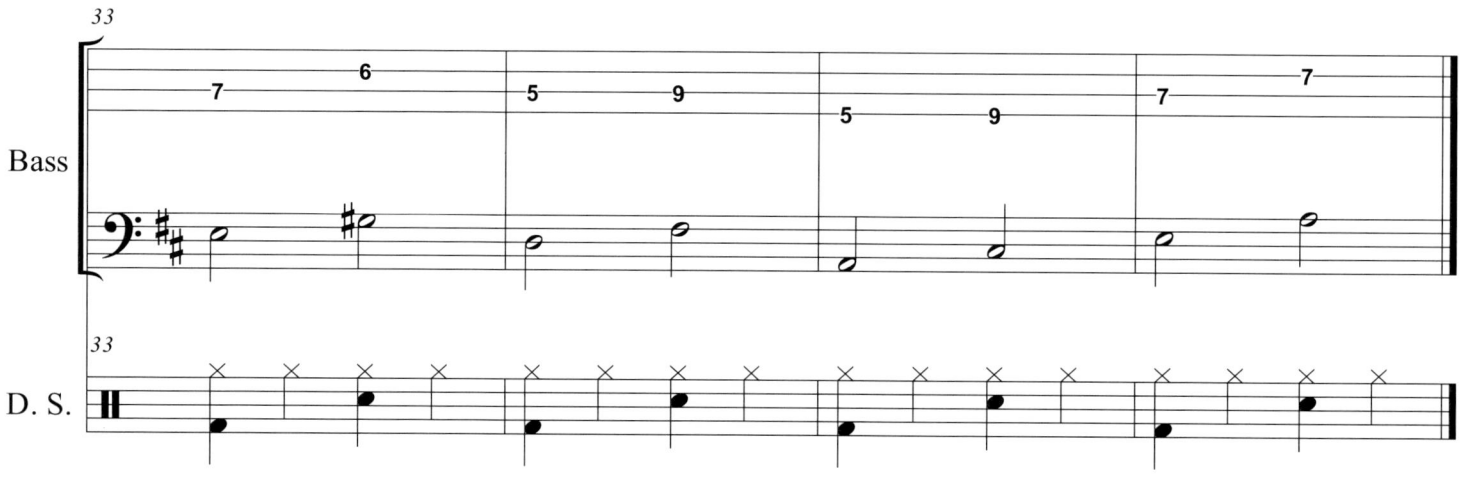

Rhythm 21

These examples are about switching feels while playing the blues. It's always important to be able to switch and color feels up during choruses in the blues. These next 3 examples show you how to switch from 4/4 to 6/8 and reverse, as well as going from 4/4 to 12/8.

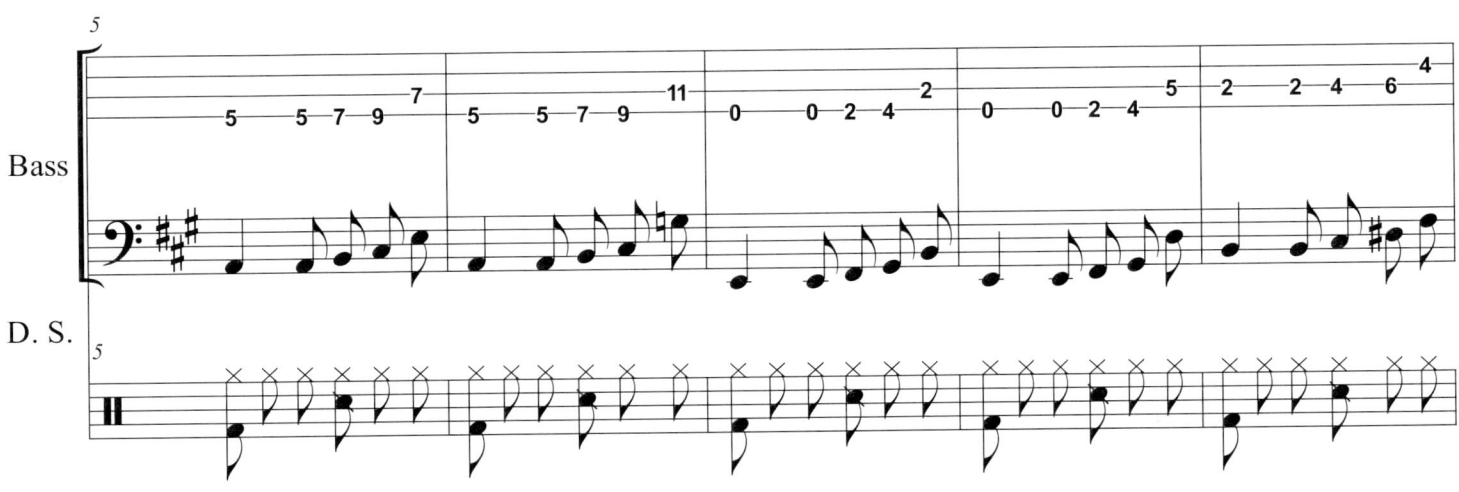

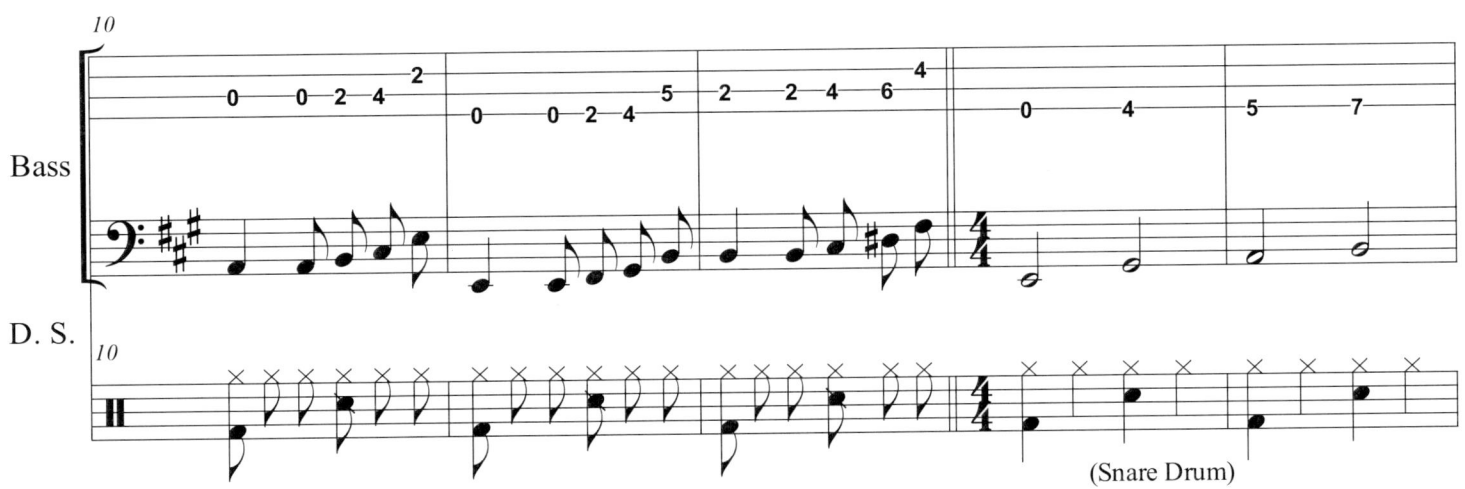

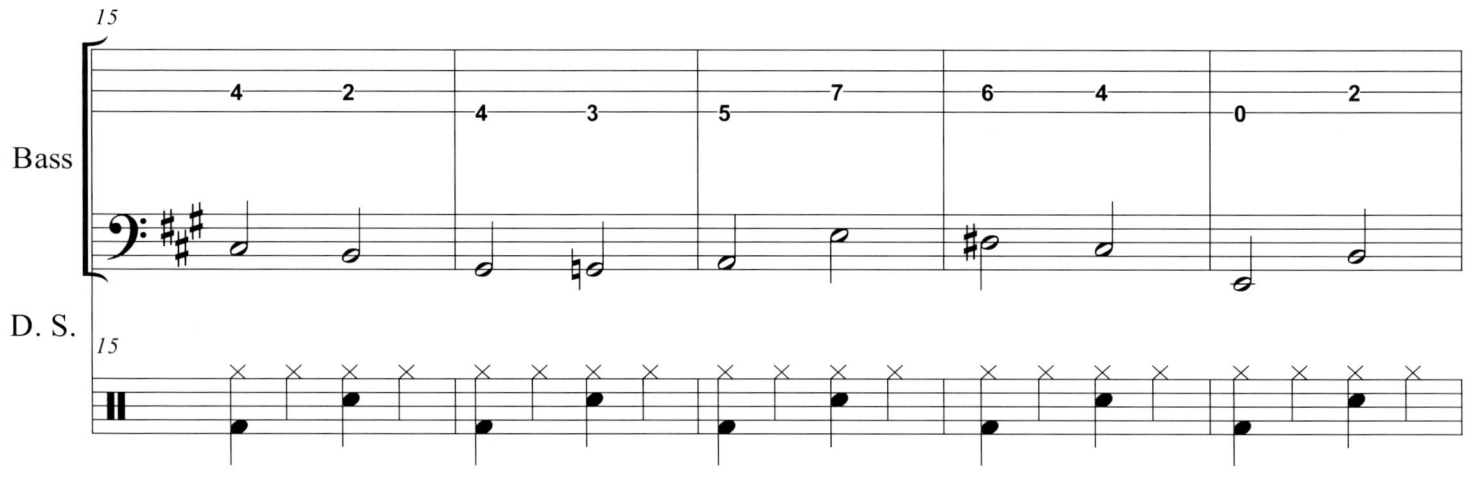
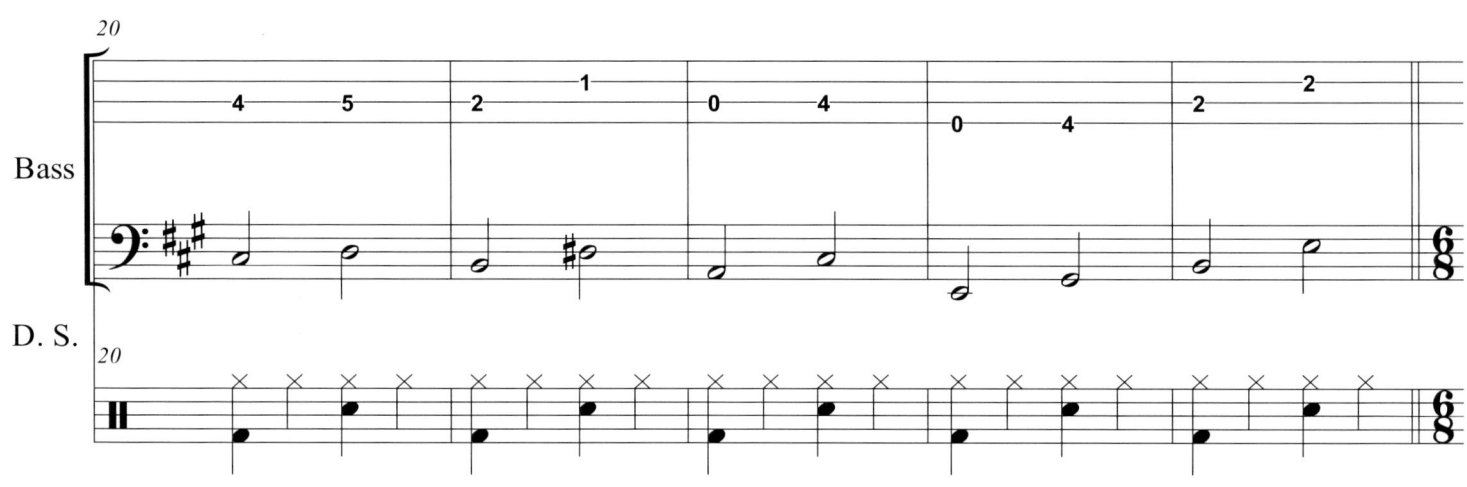
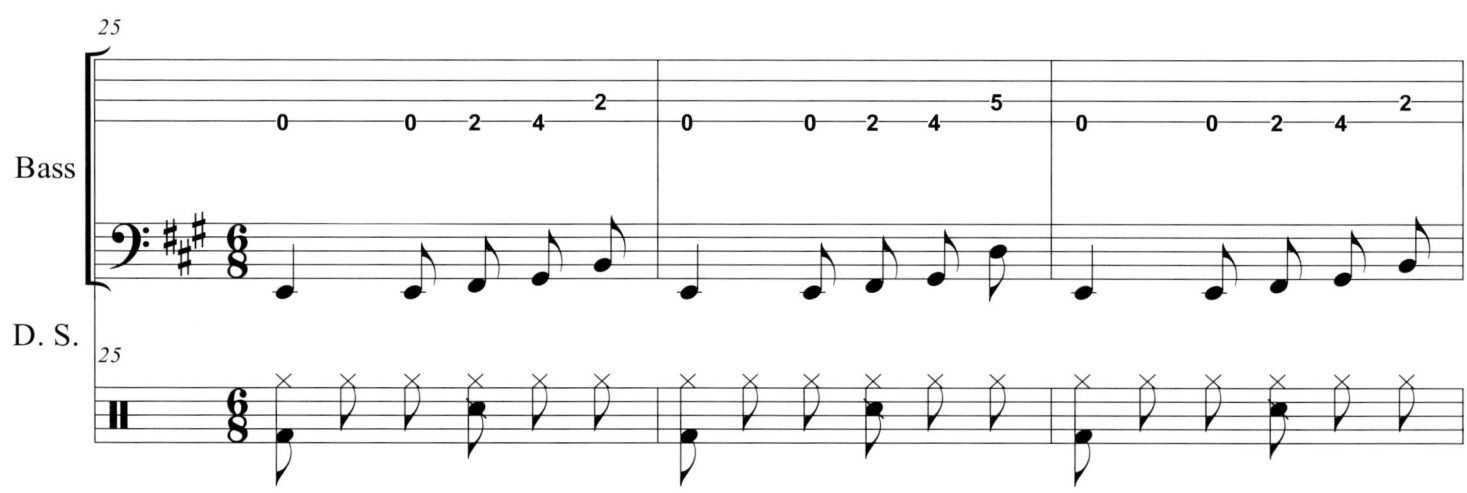

Rhythm 22

These examples are about switching feels while playing the blues. It's always important to be able to switch and color feels up during choruses in the blues. These next 3 examples show you how to switch from 4/4 to 6/8 and reverse, as well as going from 4/4 to 12/8.

Rhythm 23

Example 23 breaks into playing latin grooves. This latin feel is in 6/8 but has an underlining 4 on the floor given by the drummer. The fast tempo makes this somewhat of a tricky groove.

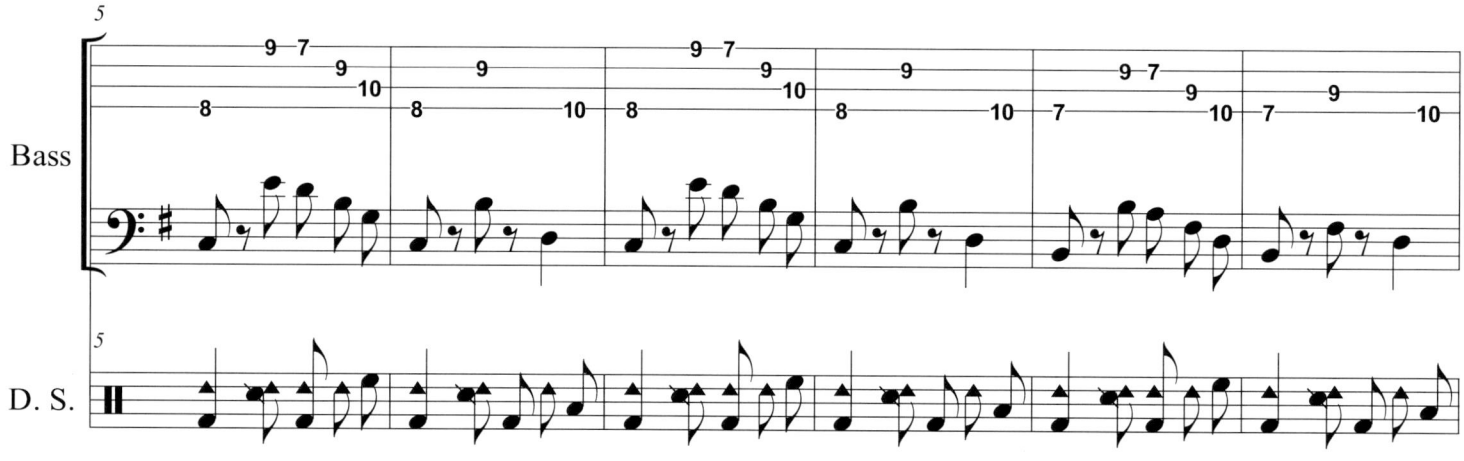

Rhythm 24

This exercise helps you focus in on both 3:2 and 2:3 clave in latin music. Both are standard claves you will see in everyday playing. Starting with the 3:2 then the middle section switches to the 2:3 clave. If you can master this, your latin pocket can expand really deeply.

Rhythm 25

Example 25 shows you how odd bar phrases in 4/4 work. With 3, 5, and 7 bar phrases being thrown in the mix, this can spice up any composition being written while still playing in 4/4.

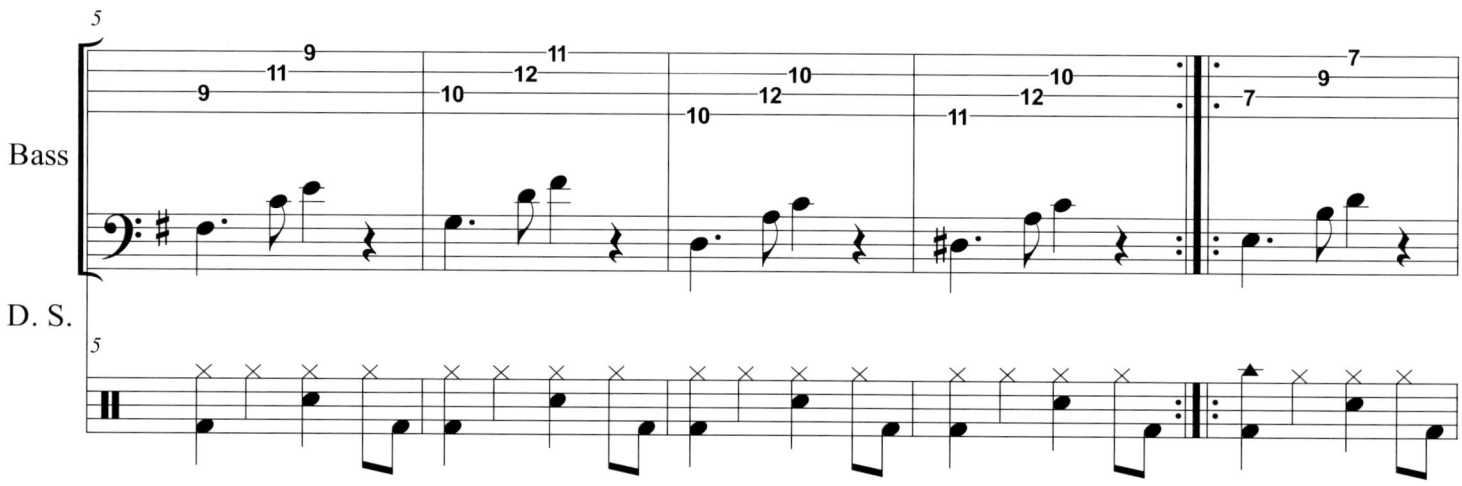
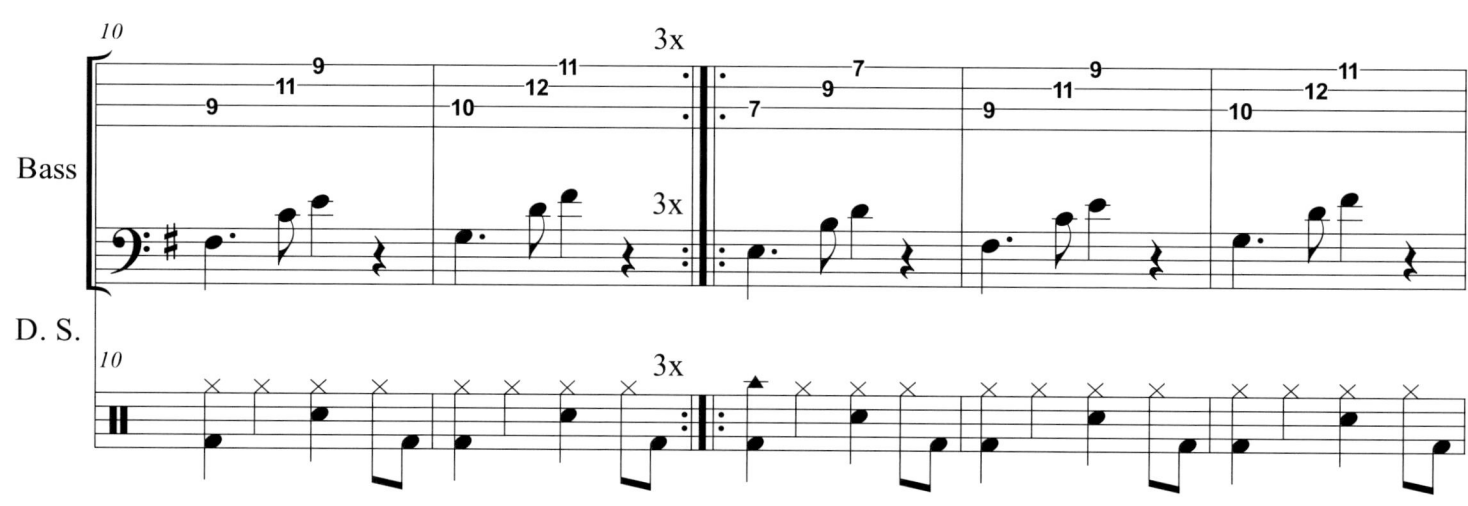

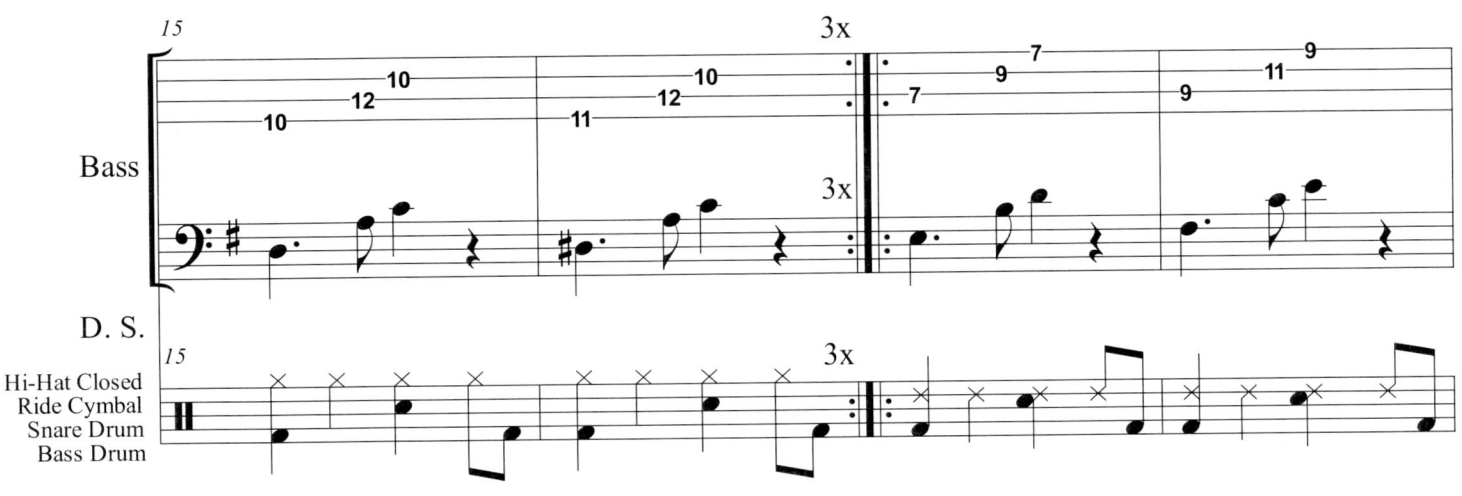

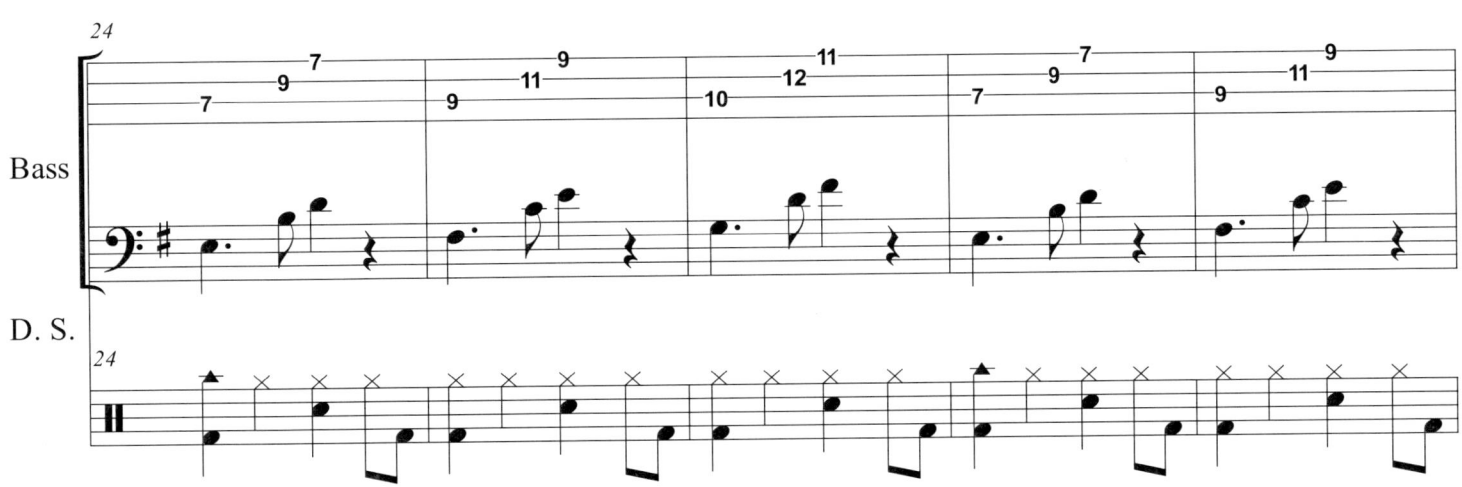

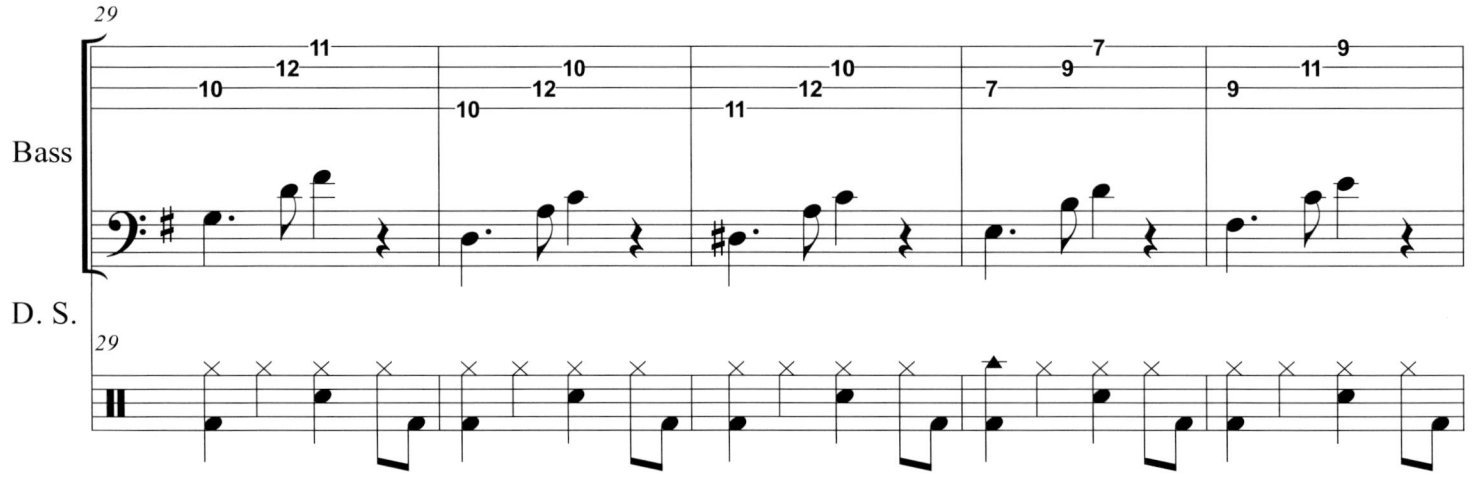
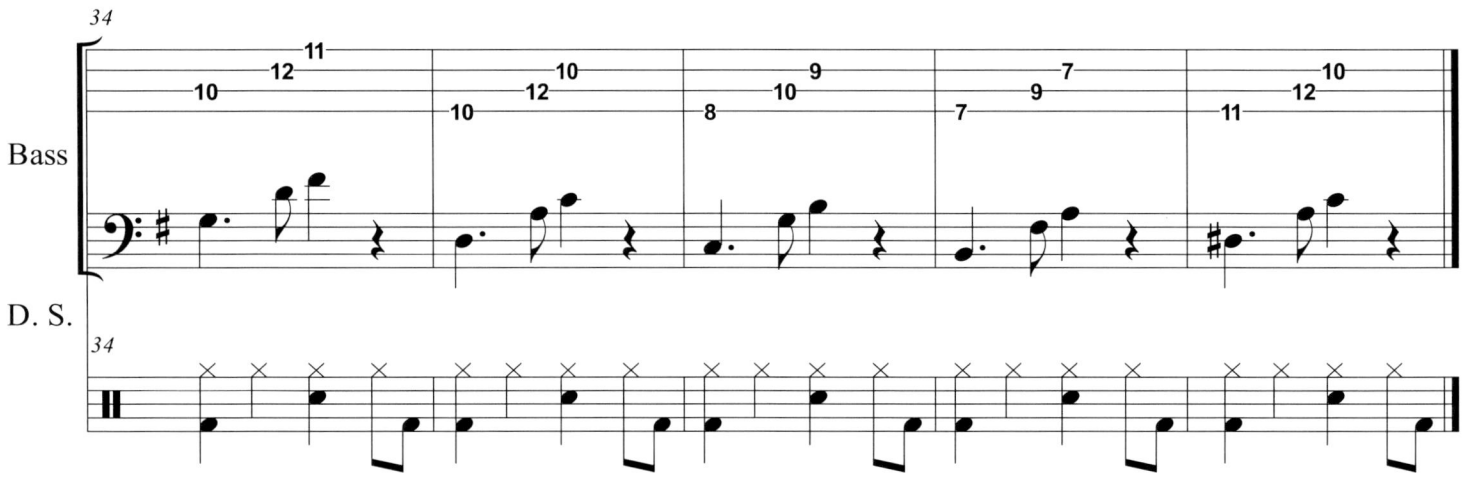

Rhythm 26

This exercise has a mix of time signatures. The base of the example is all 4/4 but thrown in the mix are one bar odd measures. It's always cool when playing in 4/4 to throw an odd bar in somewhere. This example shows you how.

Tempo 340

Rhythm 27

Example 27 is about laying down a good funky groove in 6/8. No matter if it's hip-hop or funk, being dynamic but not "busy" is important. This example has slight variations of the groove for the drummer, with the bassist keeping the same riff and filling every 4 bars.

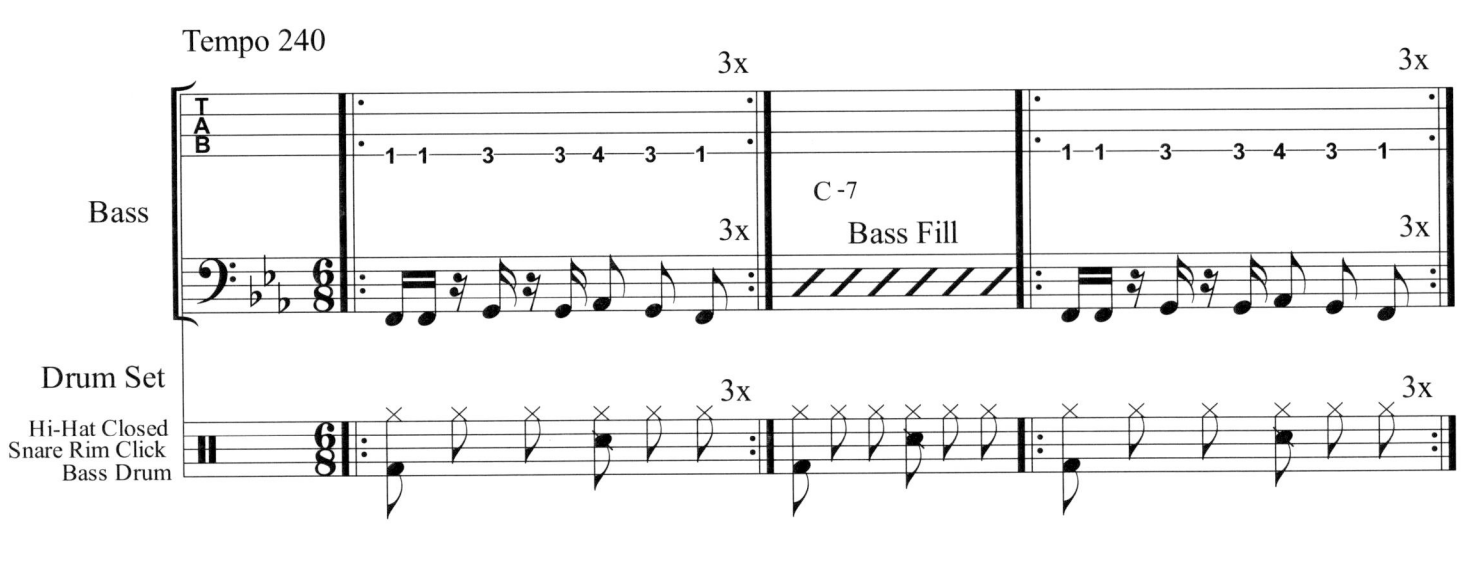

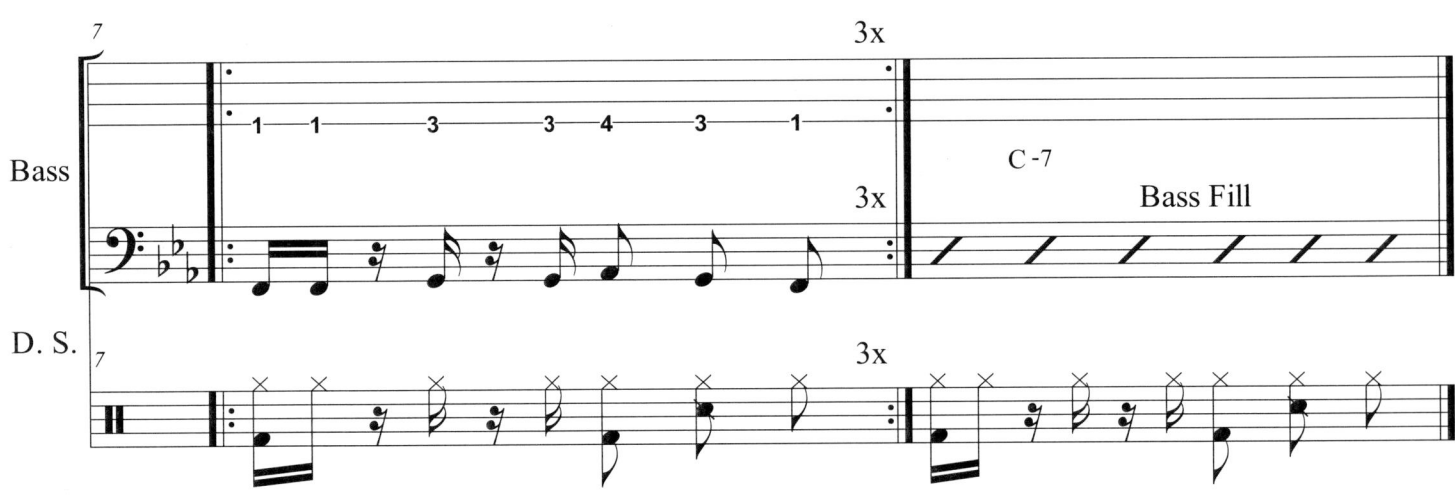

Rhythm 28

This example is about playing in 6/4. 6/4 feels great and is as common as 4/4 so being comfortable in it is important.

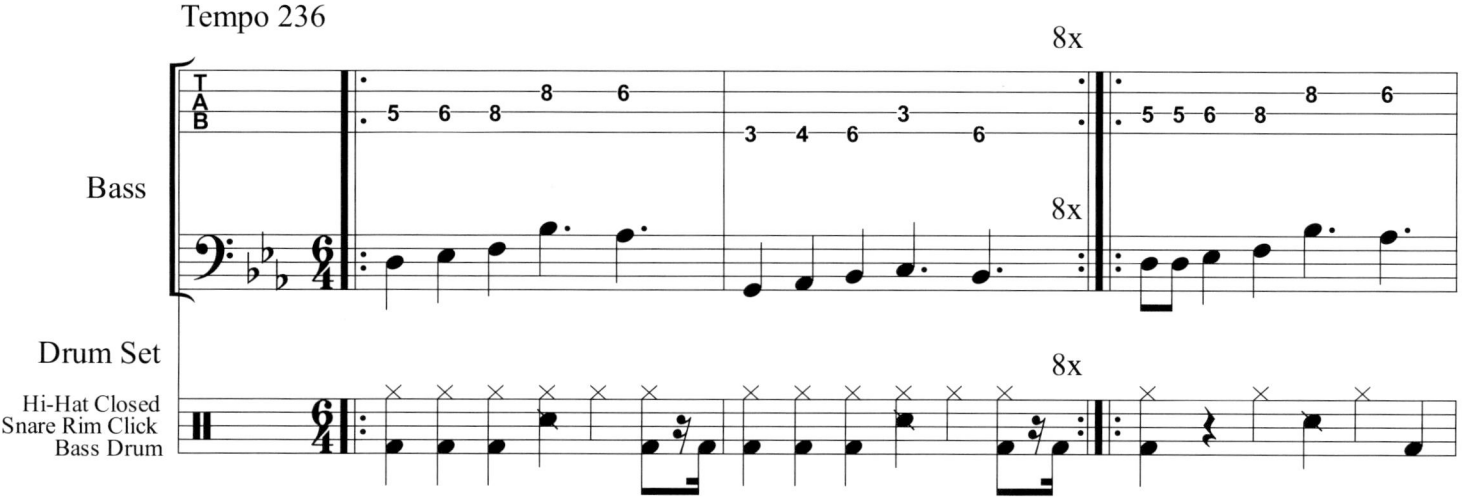

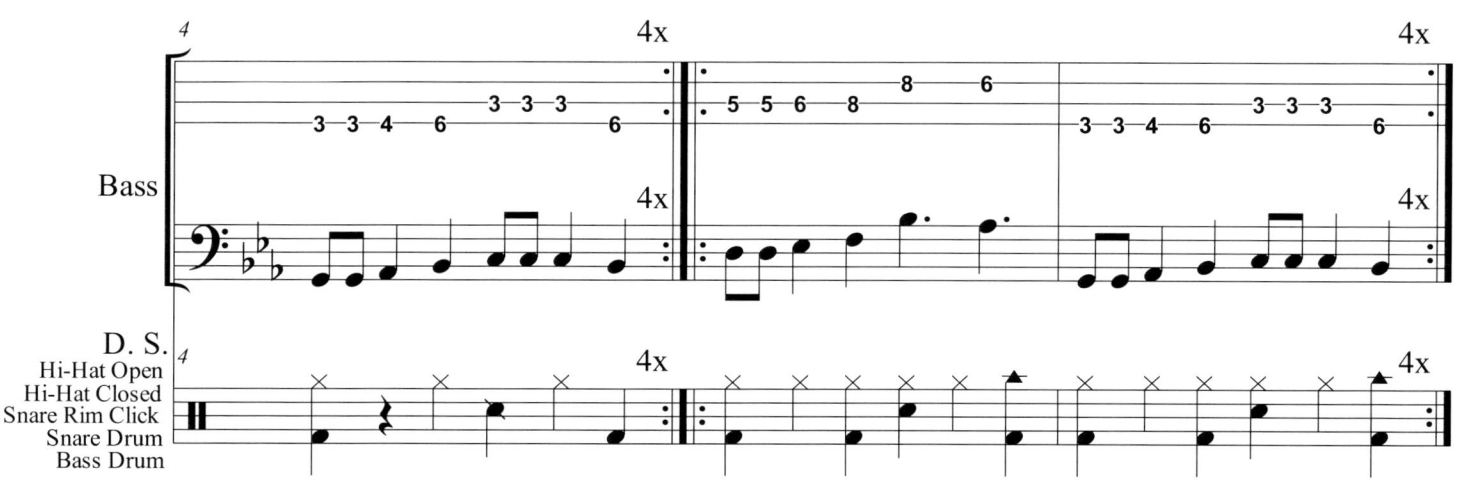

Rhythm 29

Example 29 shows you how to play the 4 in a 5/4 polyrhythm. Believe it or not you can play 4/4 inside 5/4. This example shows you what that sounds like having the drummer do it, then the bassist, then both together.

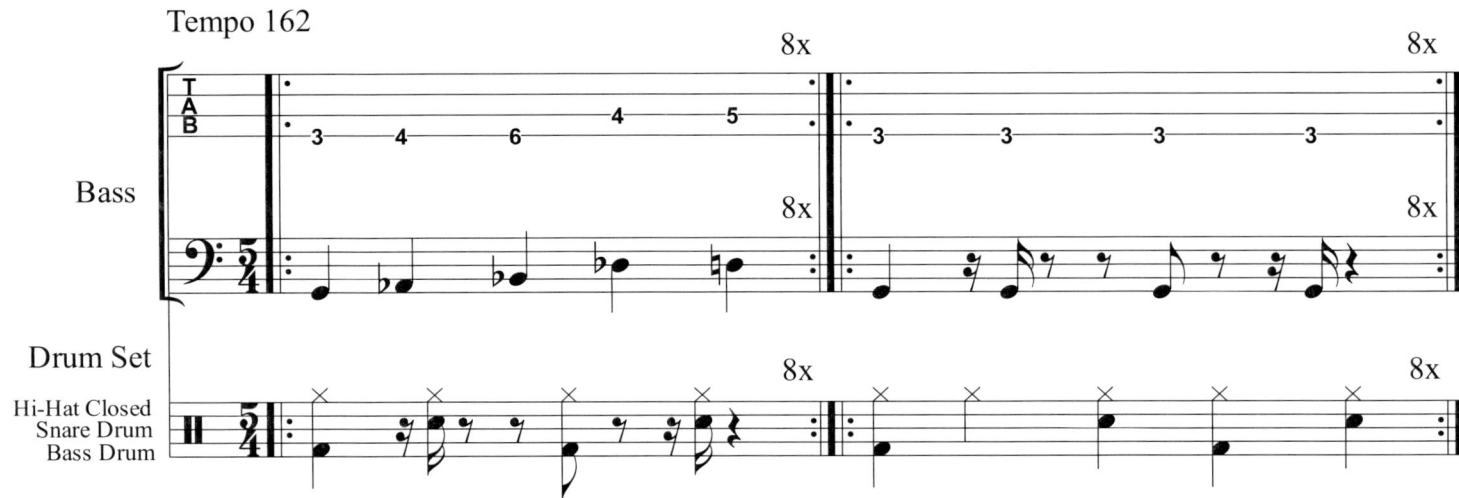

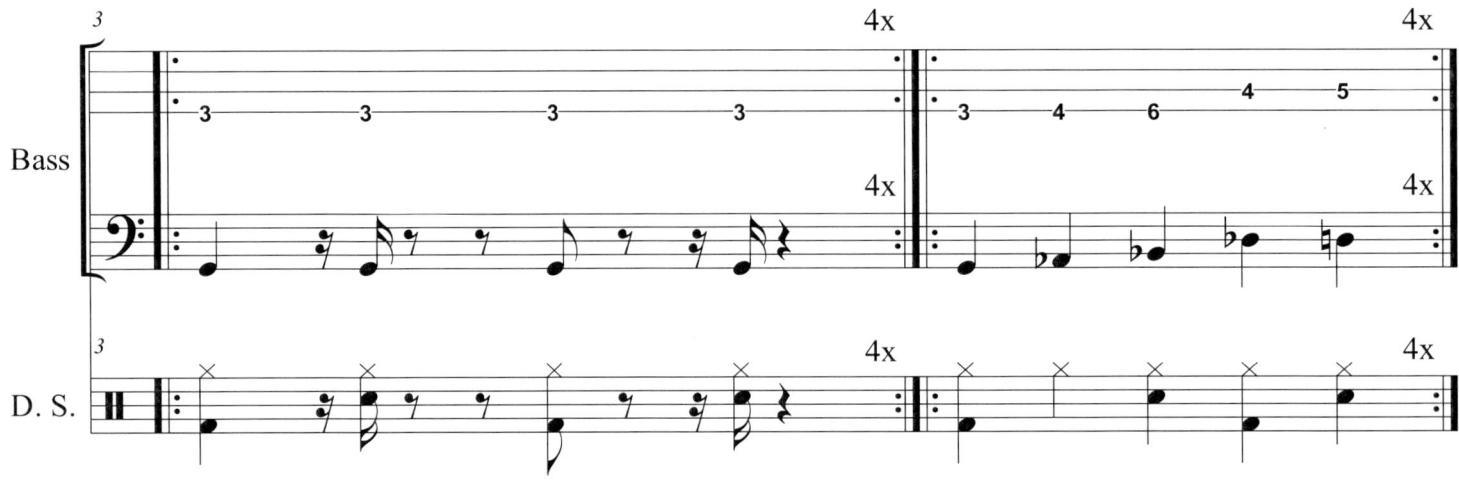

Rhythm 30

This example shows you another polyrhythm: playing 4 inside of 7/4. You can make a 4/4 groove inside of 7/4. The drummer does it first, then the bass, then they both together as done in the previous example.

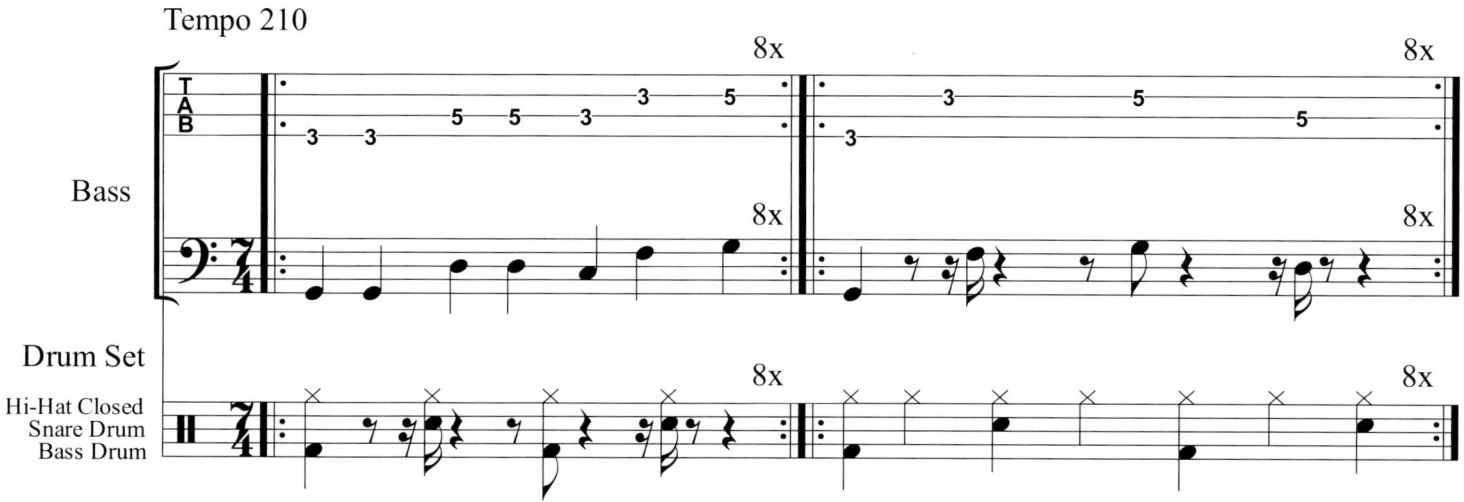

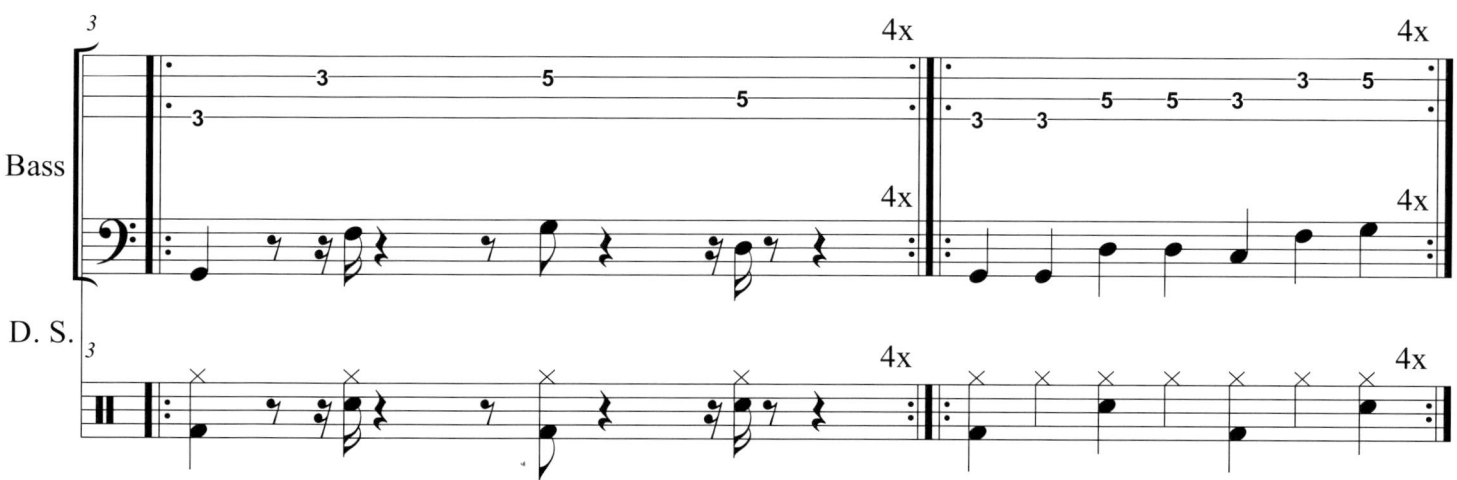

Rhythm 31

Example 31 is about grooving in 9/4. When playing in in rock context playing in different time signatures is very cool and may be used a bunch. Having the skills to play and compose in odd time gives you a wider range in where your music can go.

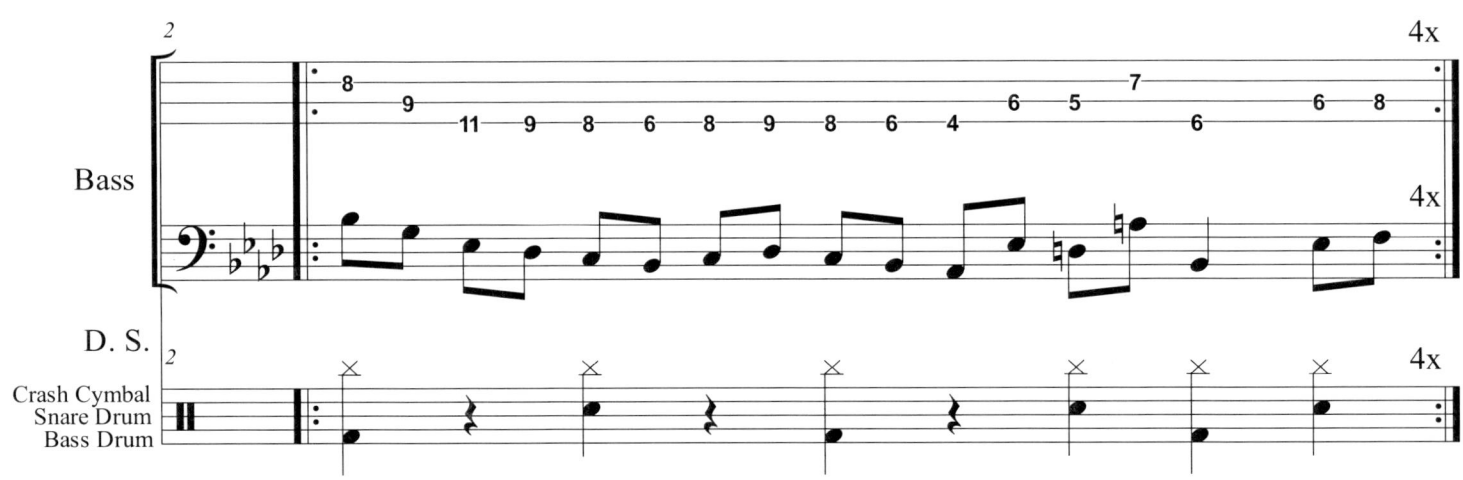

Rhythm 32

This example shows you one way of feeling 9/8: 3-3-3 giving you a triplet bounce feel. This can be great for hip-hop/funk music.

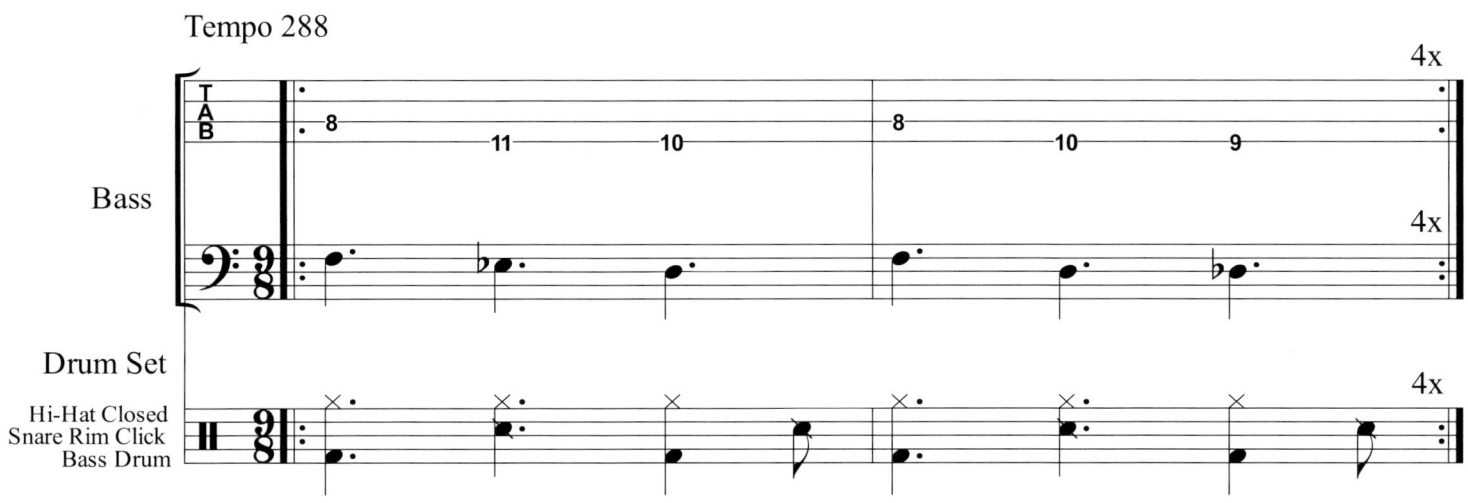

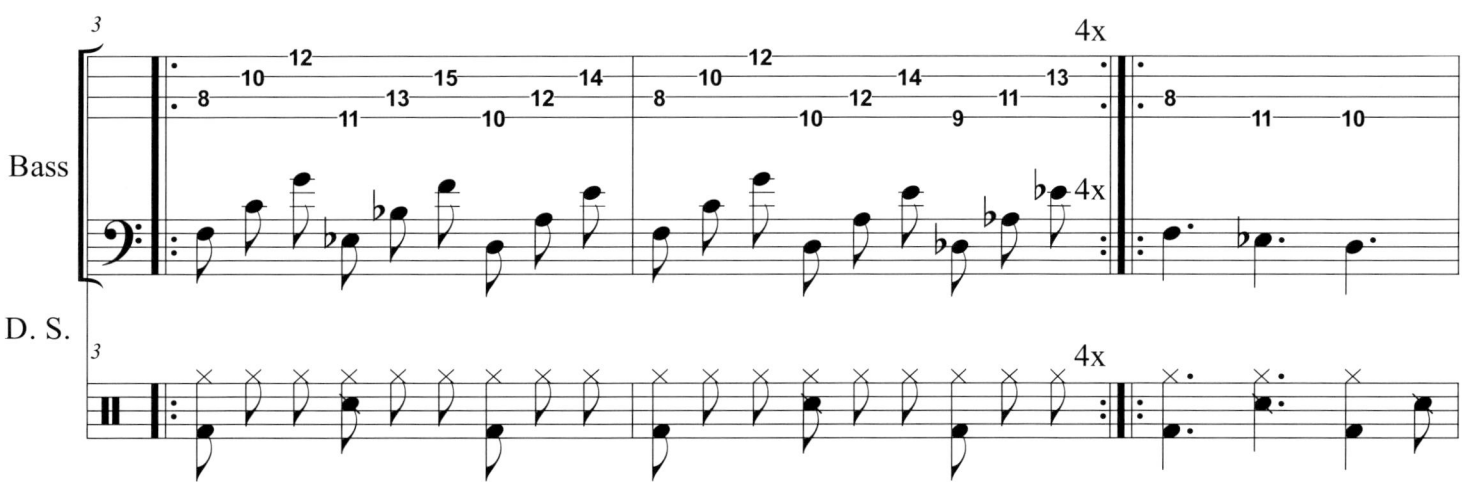

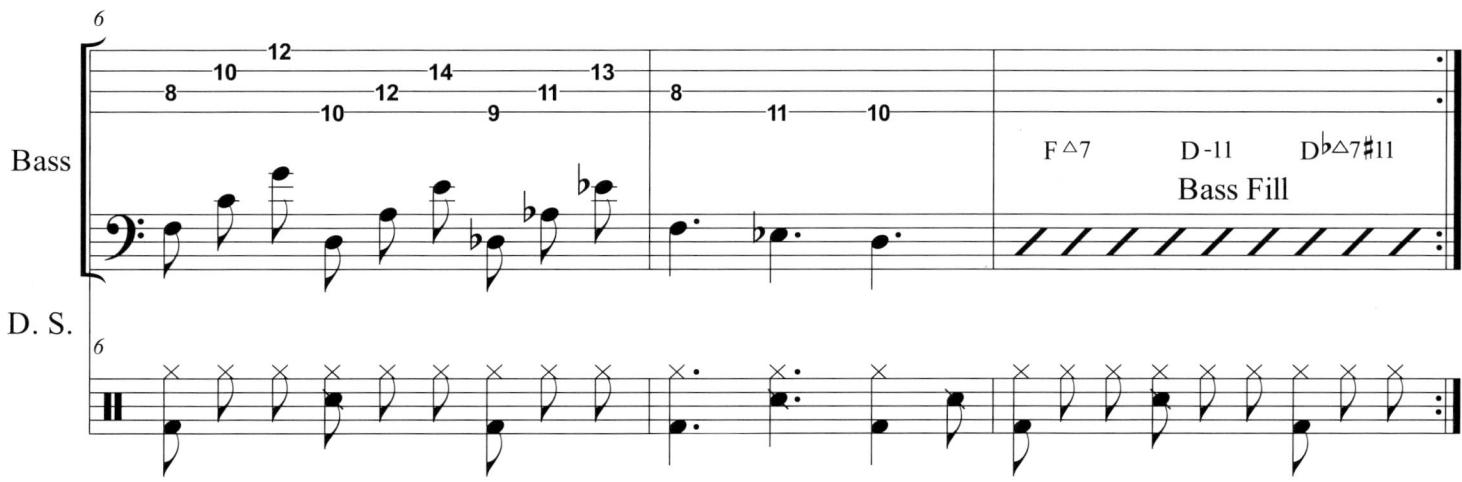

Track 33

Rhythm 33

This exercise again grooves in 9/8 but breaks it up in 5-4. This is another cool way of feeling 9/8.

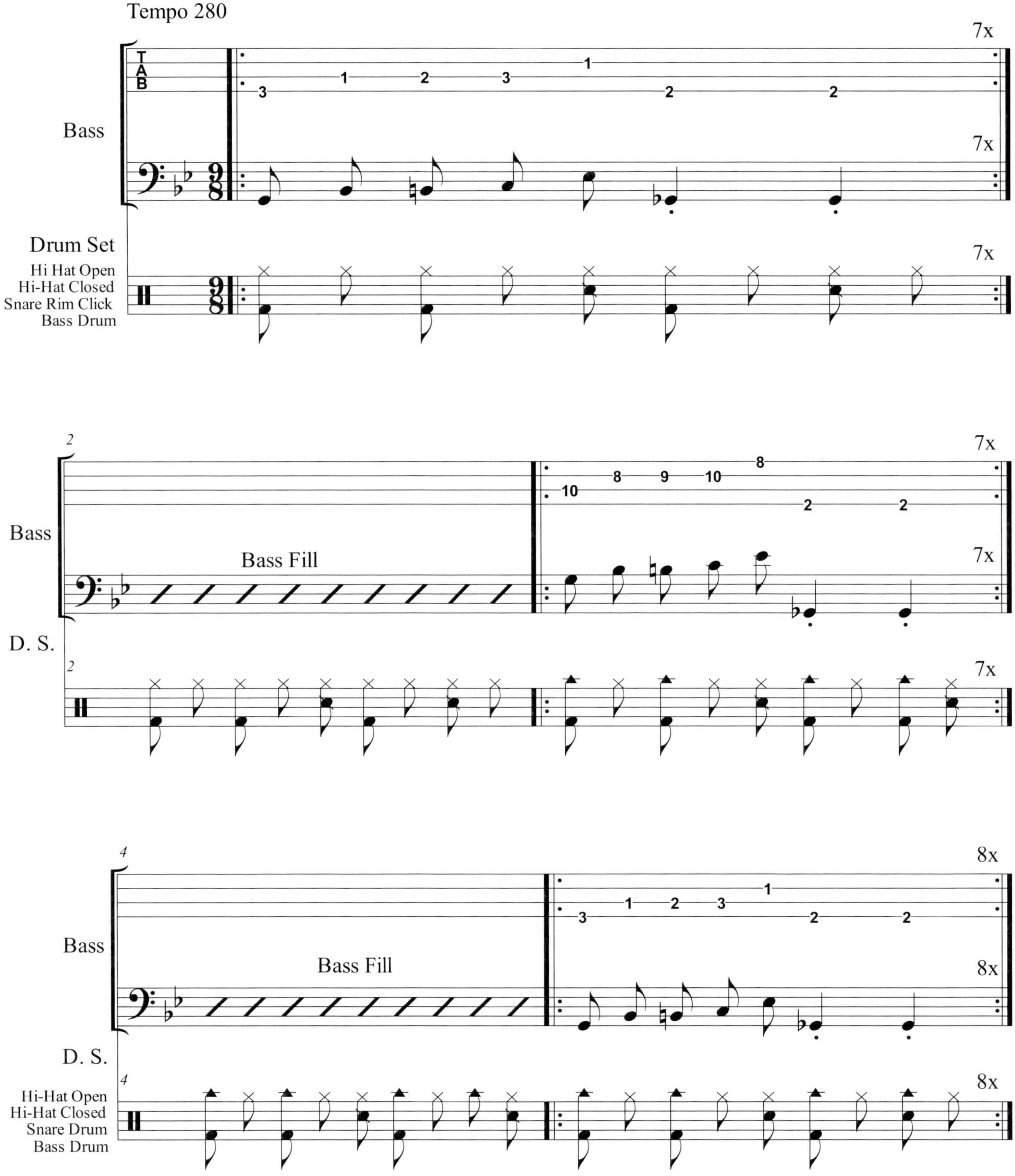

Rhythm 34

Example 34 breaks down playing 11/8. The way it's felt in this example is 7-4. This can be great for playing up-tempo rock riffs.

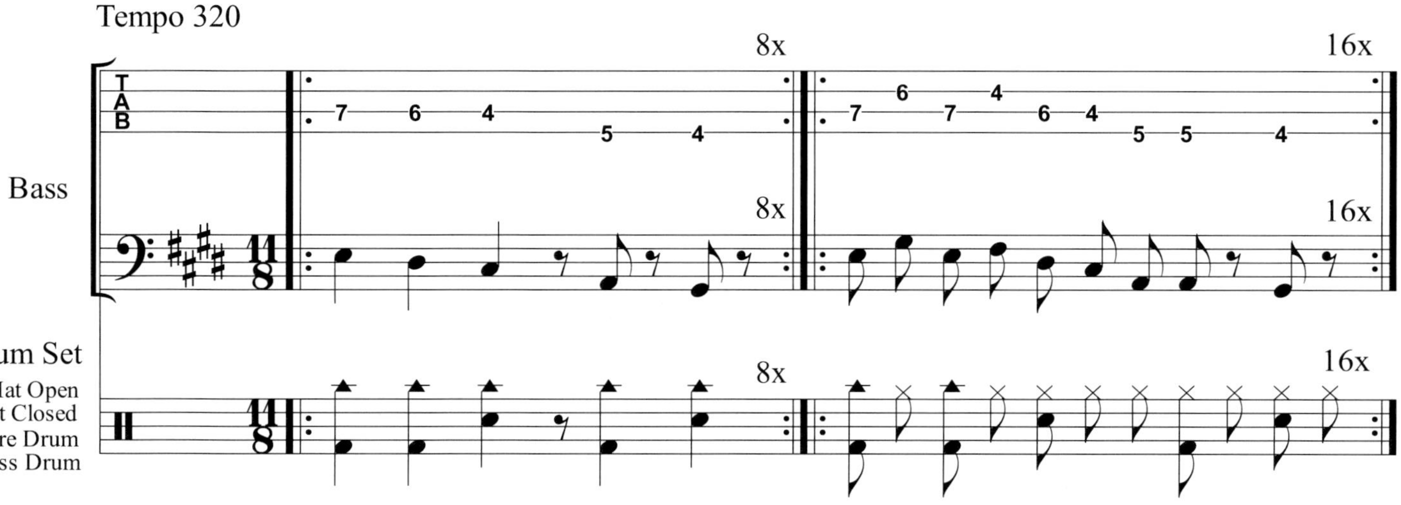

Tempo 320

Rhythm 35

This example also is in 11/8, however it is felt 6-5. This also makes for a cool rock feel. Being able to feel 11/8 different ways can come in handy.

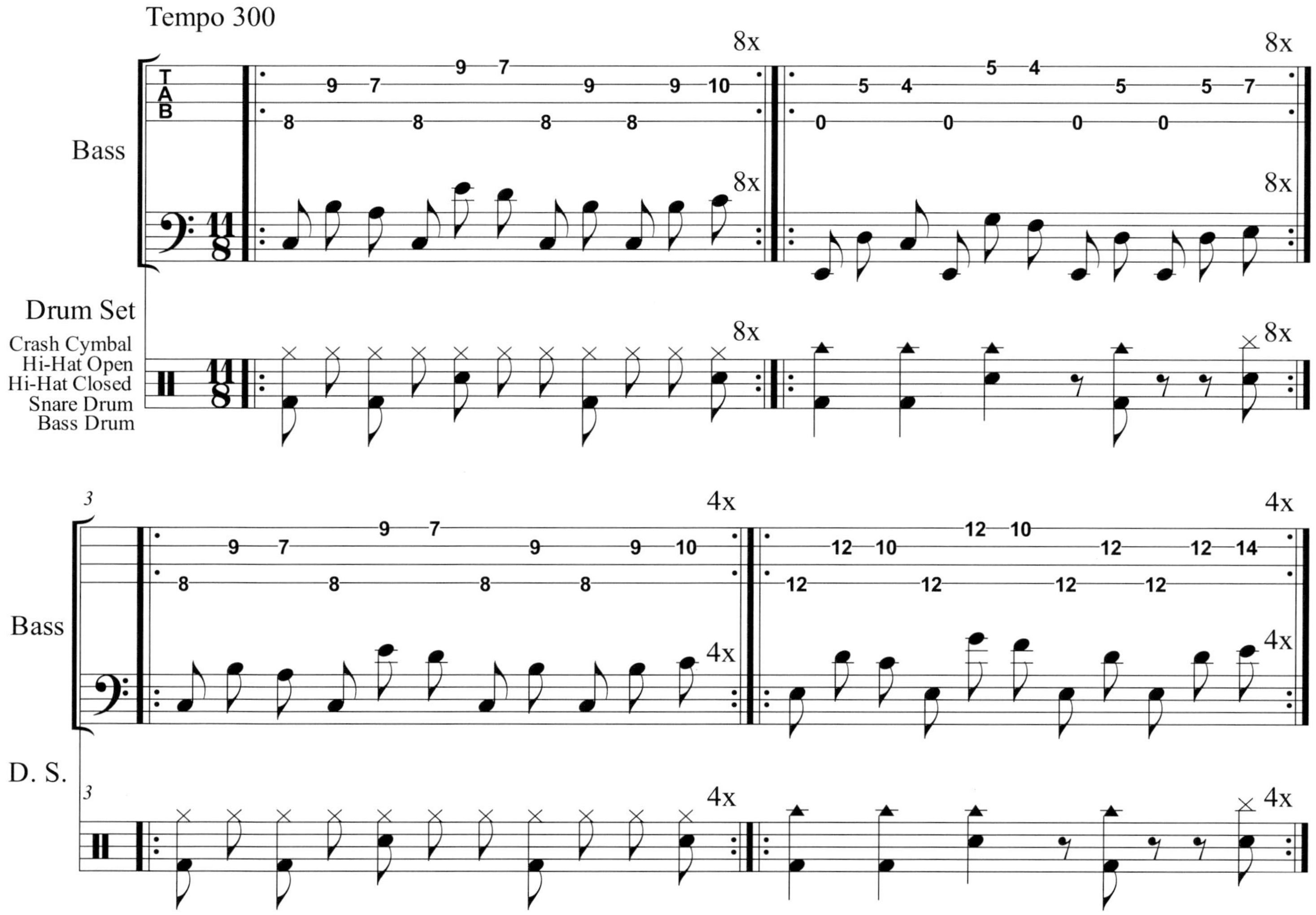

Tempo 300

47

Rhythm 36

This example shows you how to breakdown 11/8 into 5-6. Having the drummer color in the steady rock riff set by the bassist.

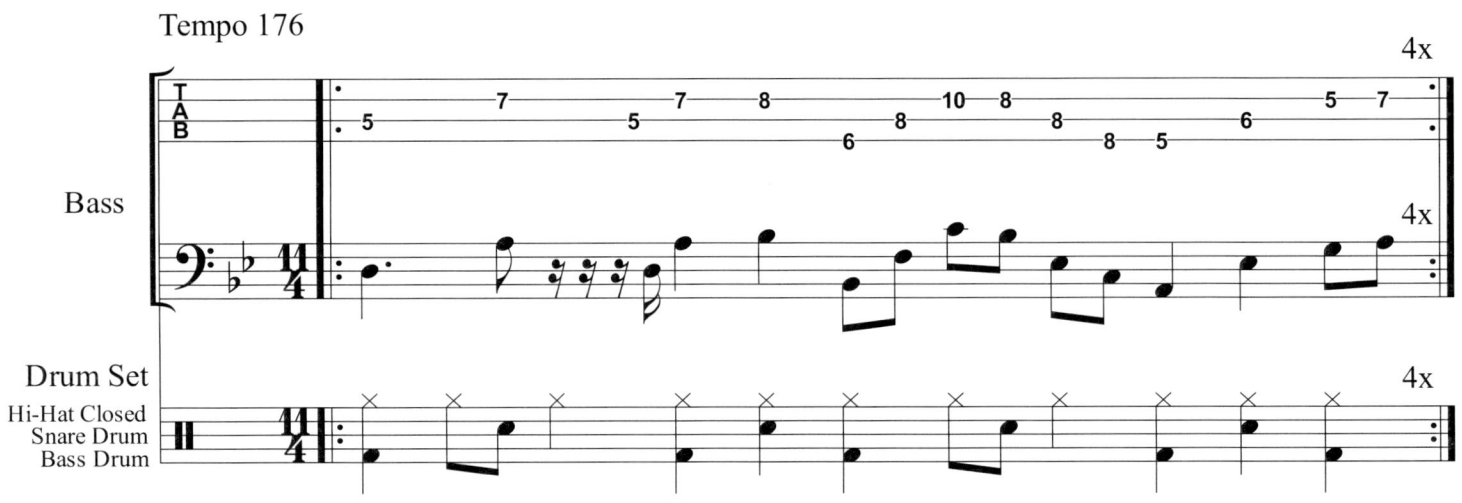

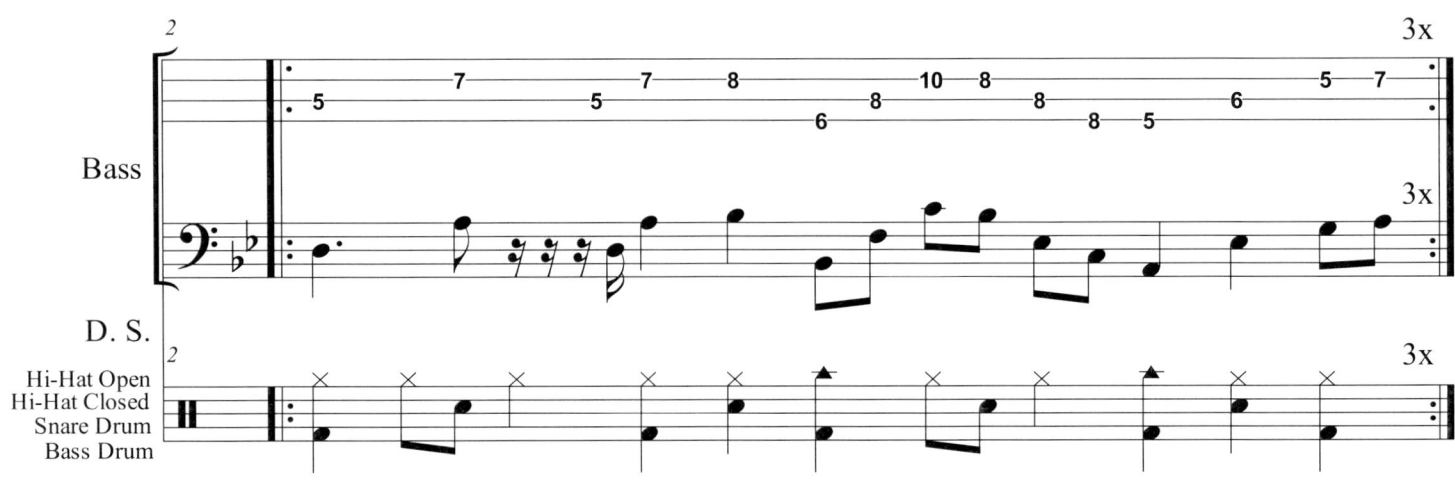

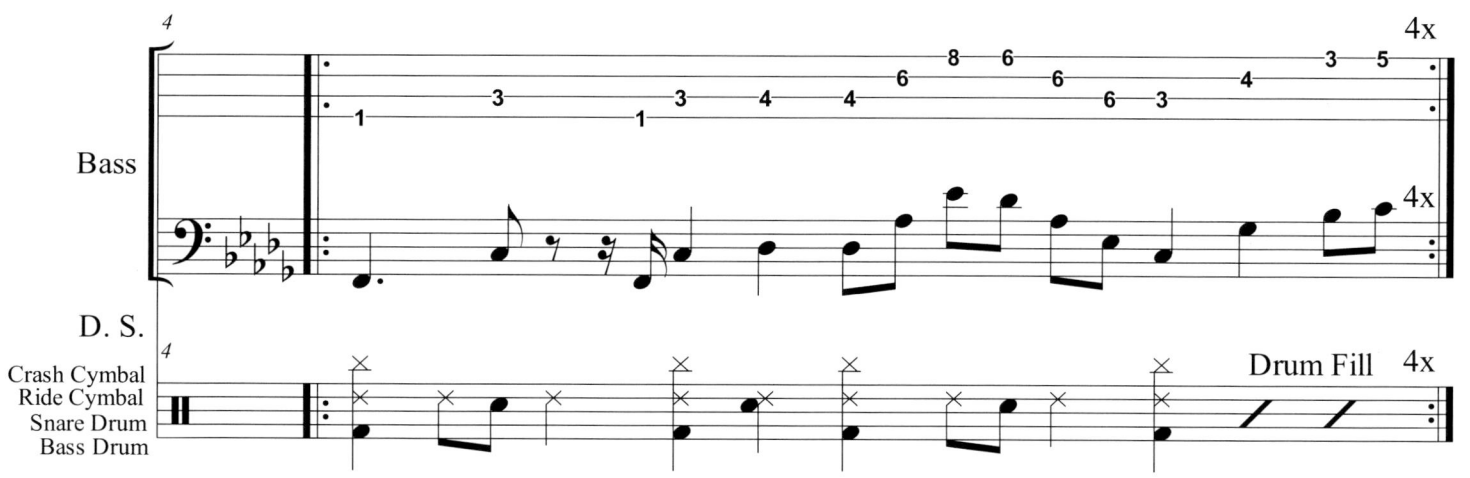

Rhythm 37

Example 37 breaks down grooving in 13/4. This example is felt 6-7. Along with the others this is just another way of feeling odd time.

Rhythm 38

Example 38 breaks down 13/8. It is broken down into 3-4-3-3. When having so many beats such as 13 it can be really cool to focus on the inner ways the time is broken up. Getting creative in that space is what's most important when dealing with big odd time bars.

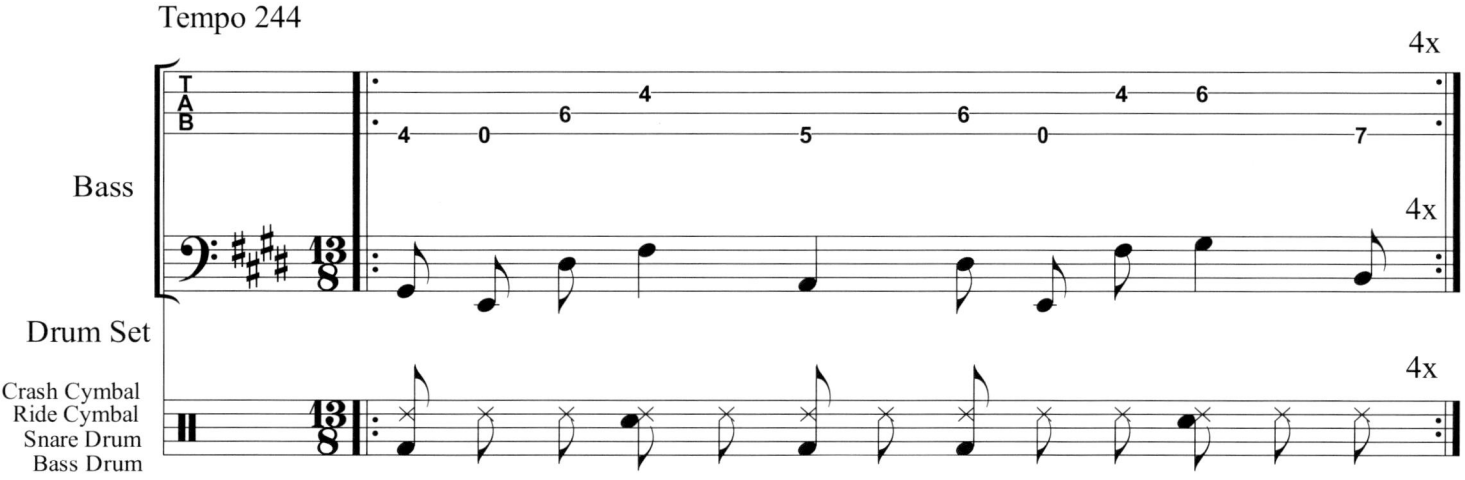

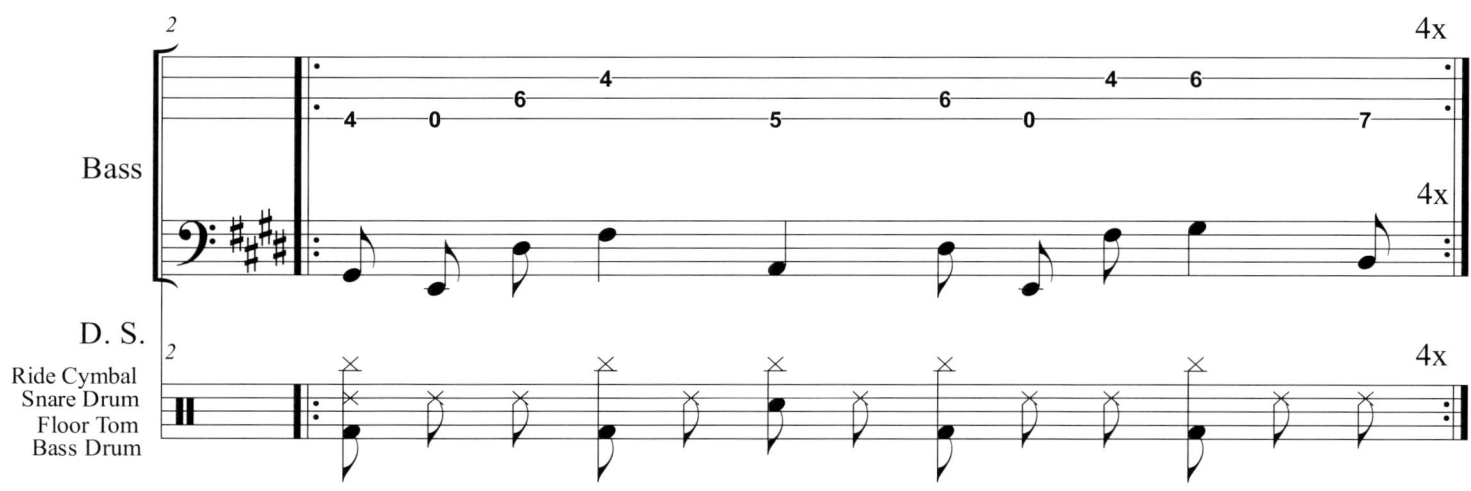

Rhythm 39

This example again breaks down 13/8. This time breaking it into 3-3-3-4. This makes for a great hip hop or funk feel.

Rhythm 40

Examples 40-48 will now be a mix of odd times and feels all thrown at you at random. The goal by now is to see a bunch of changing bars back to back and be ok playing and reading anything that comes at you. ENJOY!

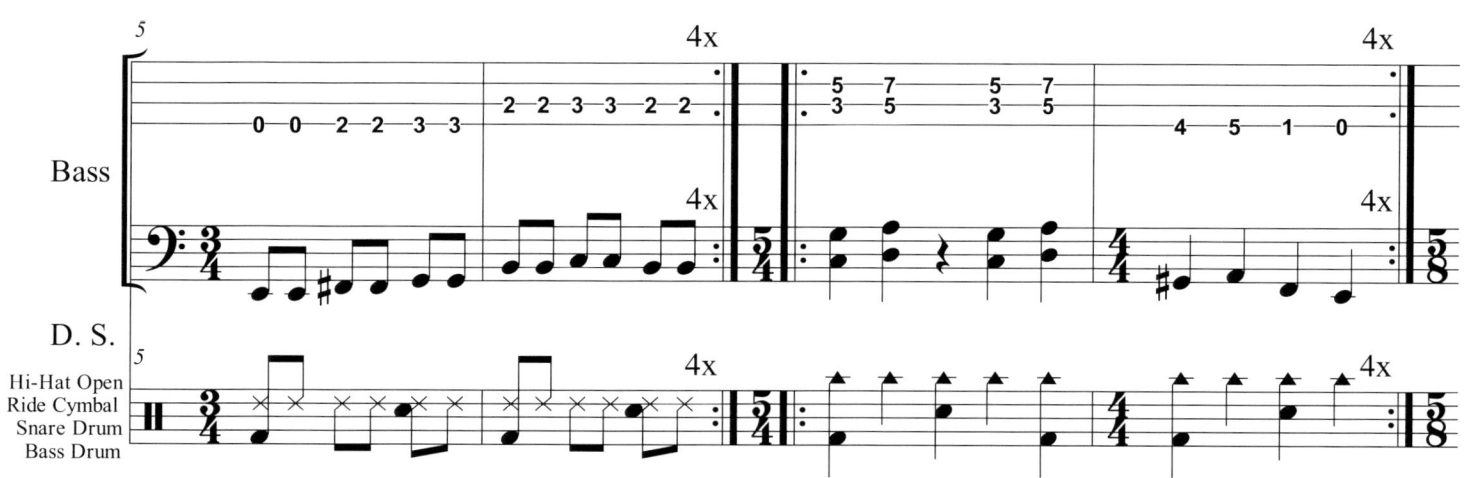

Rhythm 41

Rhythm 42

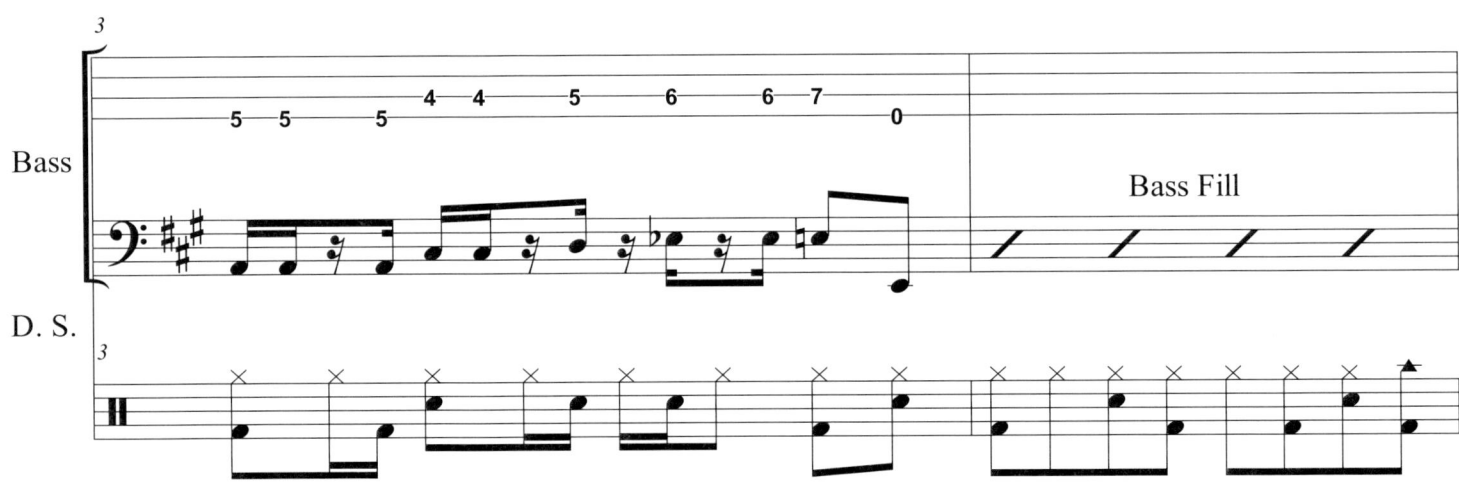

Rhythm 43

Tempo 170

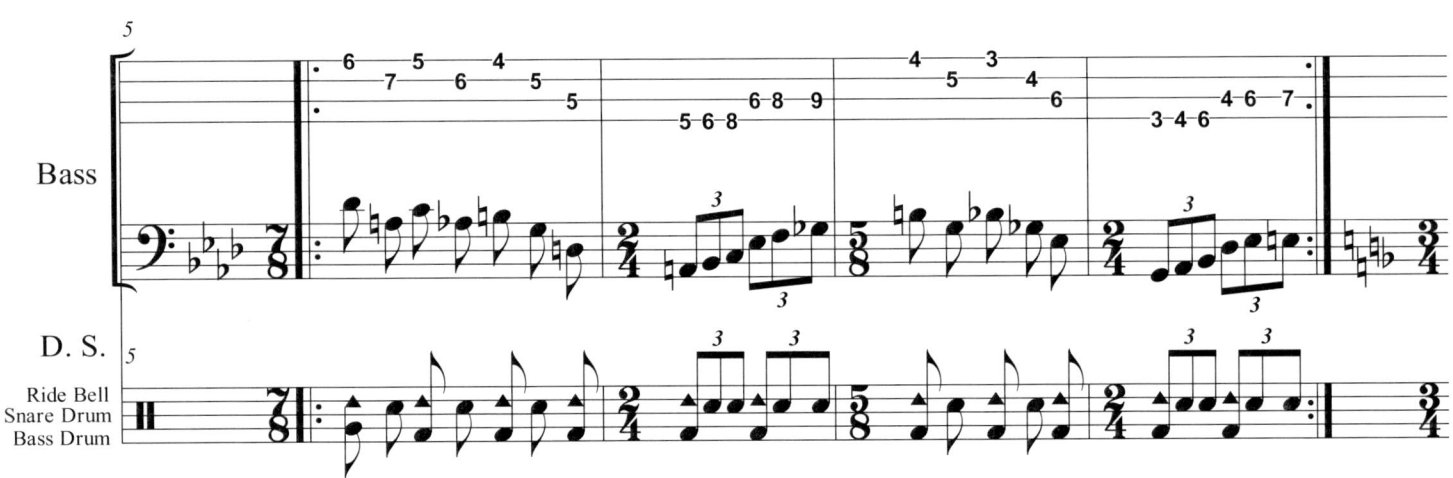

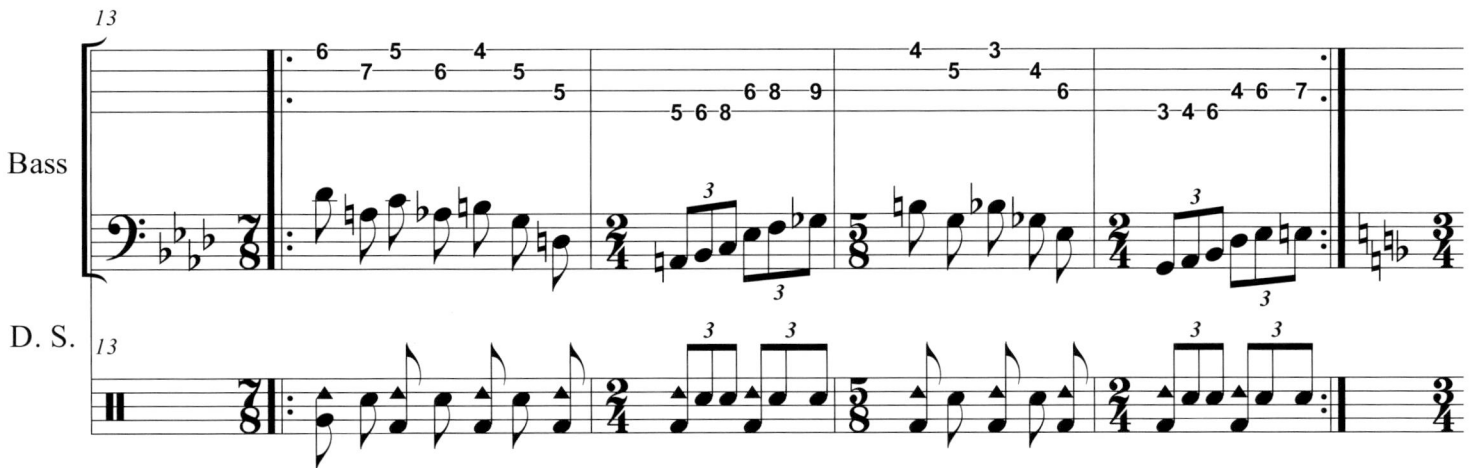

Rhythm 44

Rhythm 45

Tempo 98

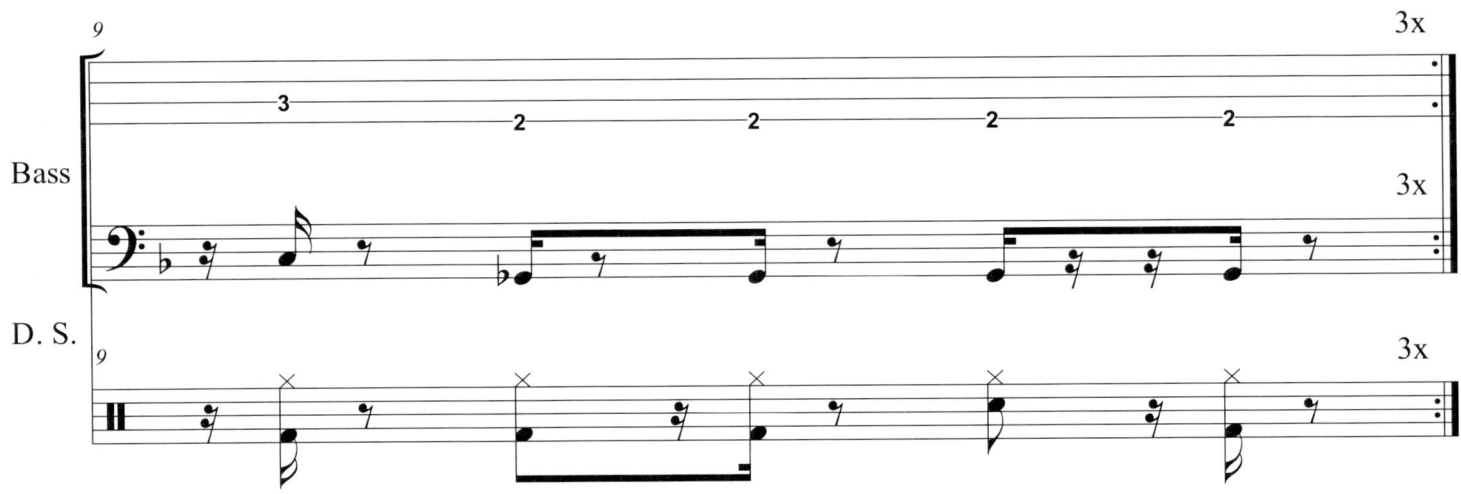

Rhythm 46

Tempo 280

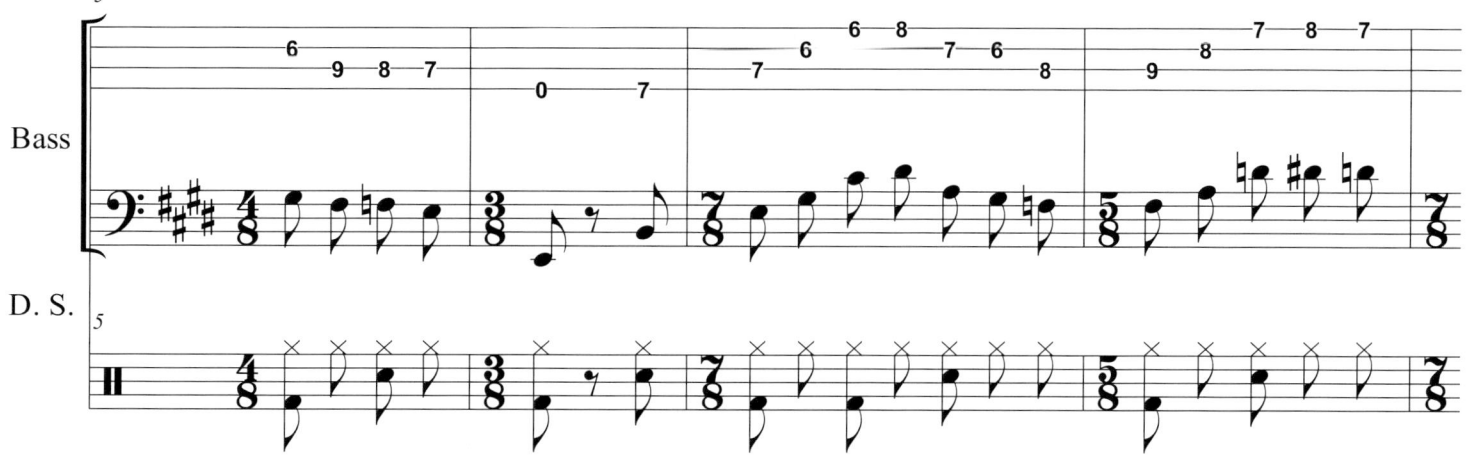

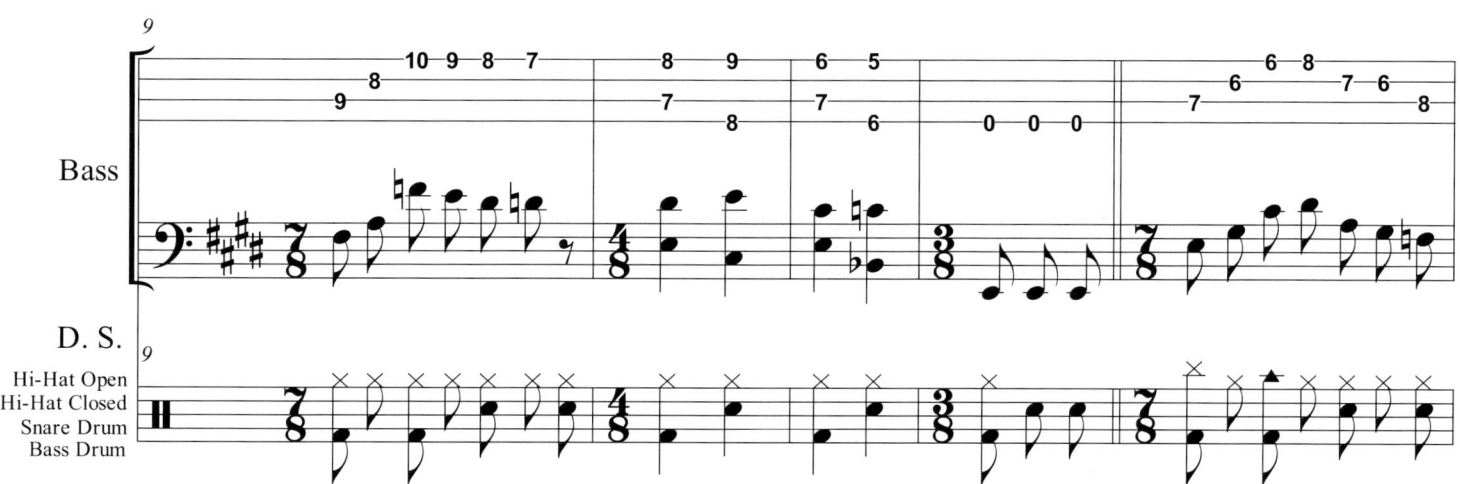

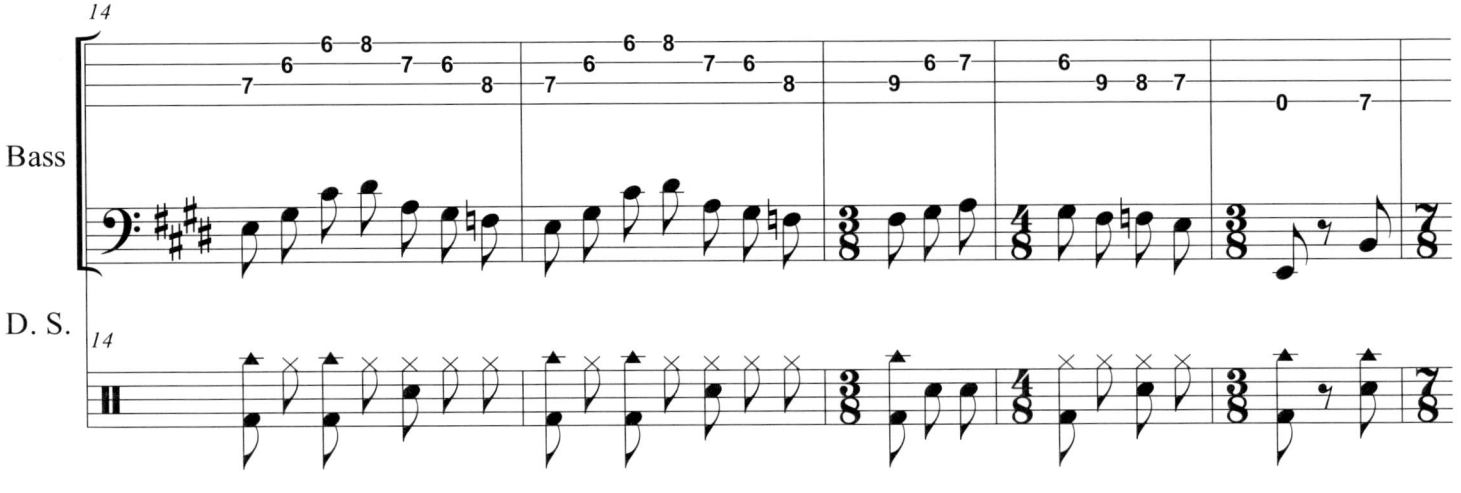

Rhythm 47

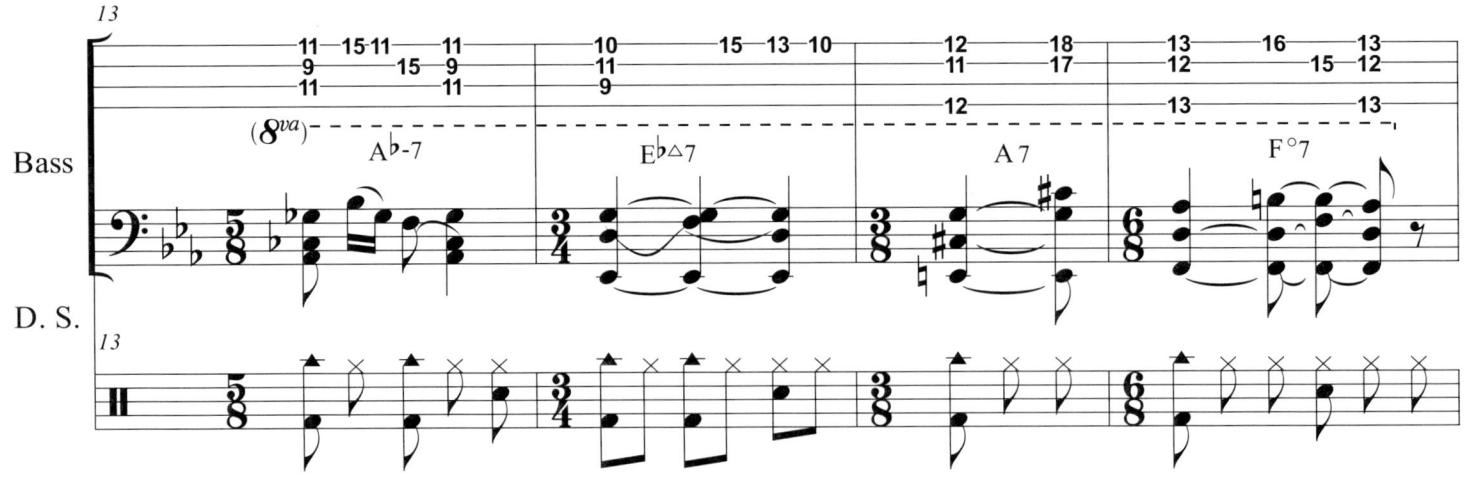
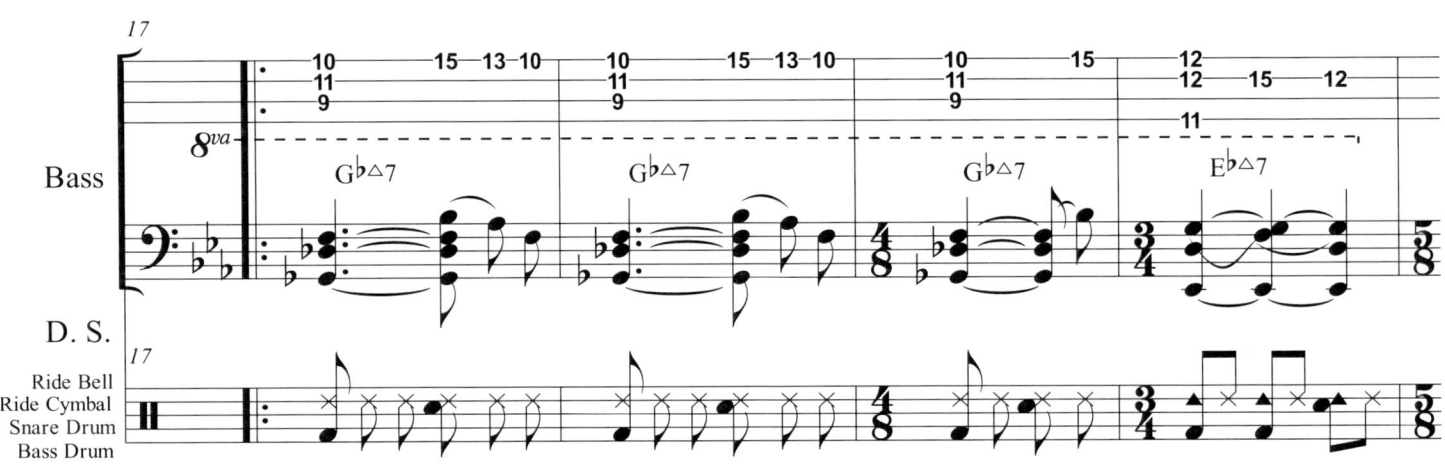
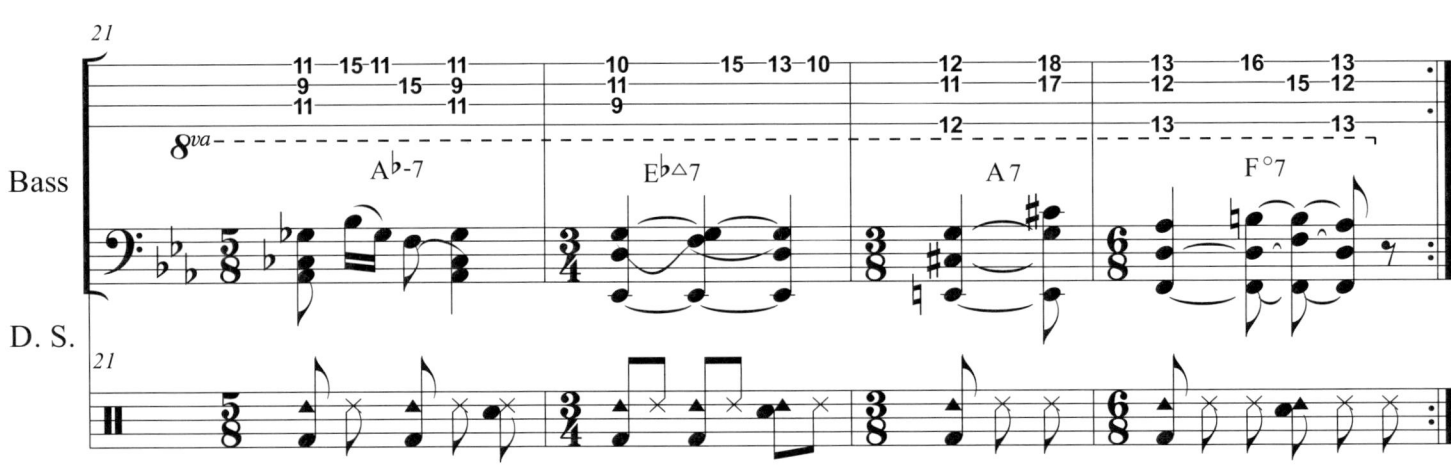

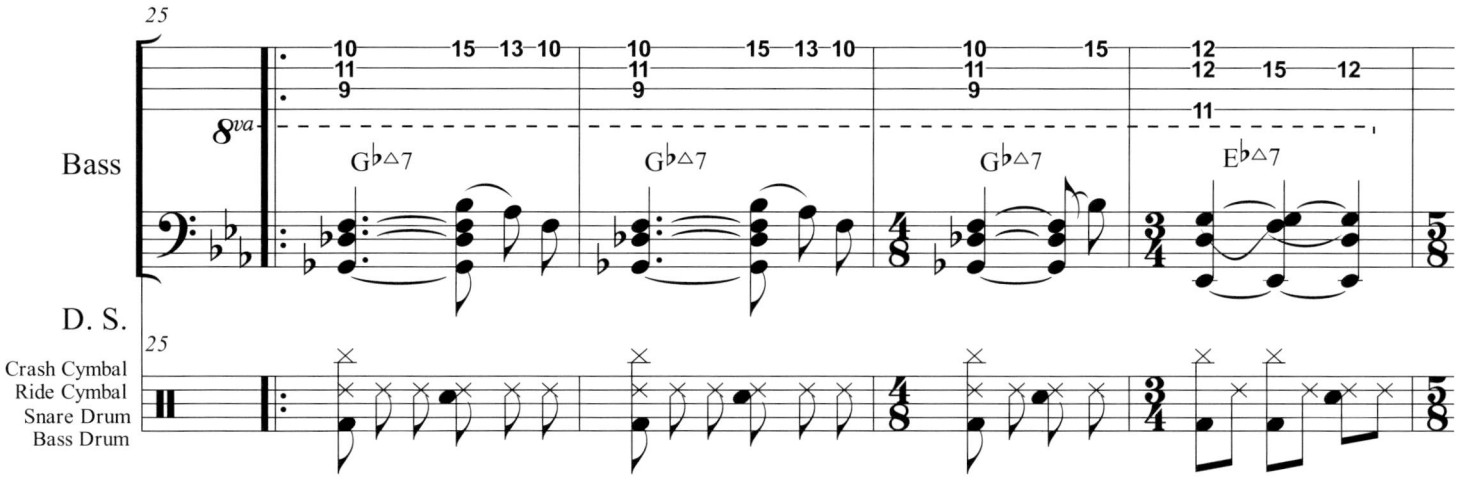
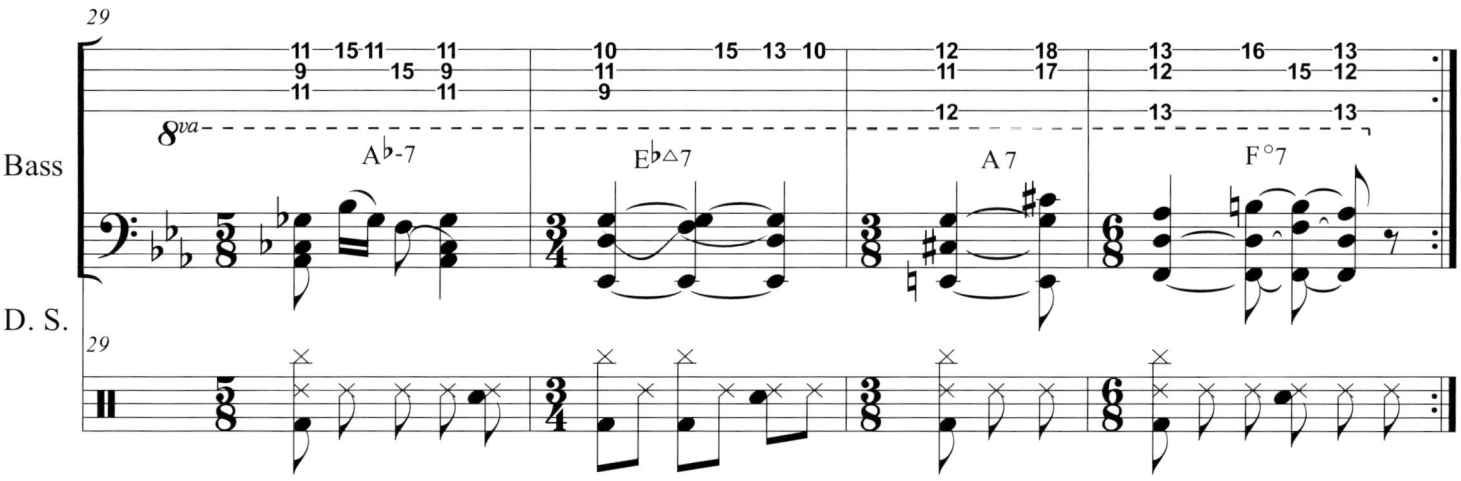

Rhythm 48

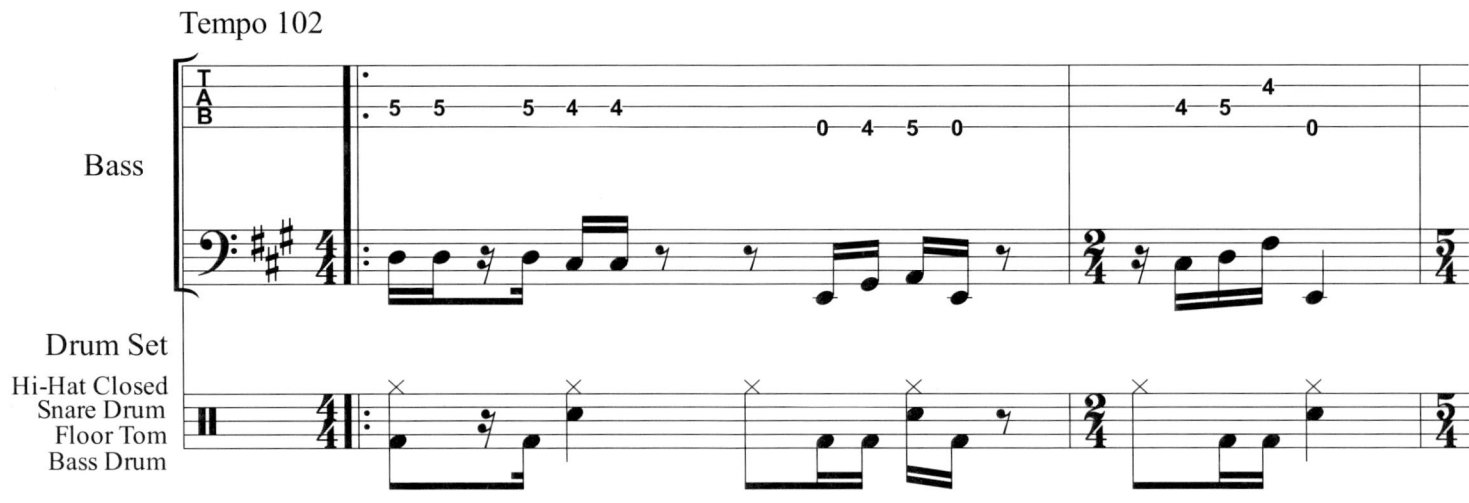

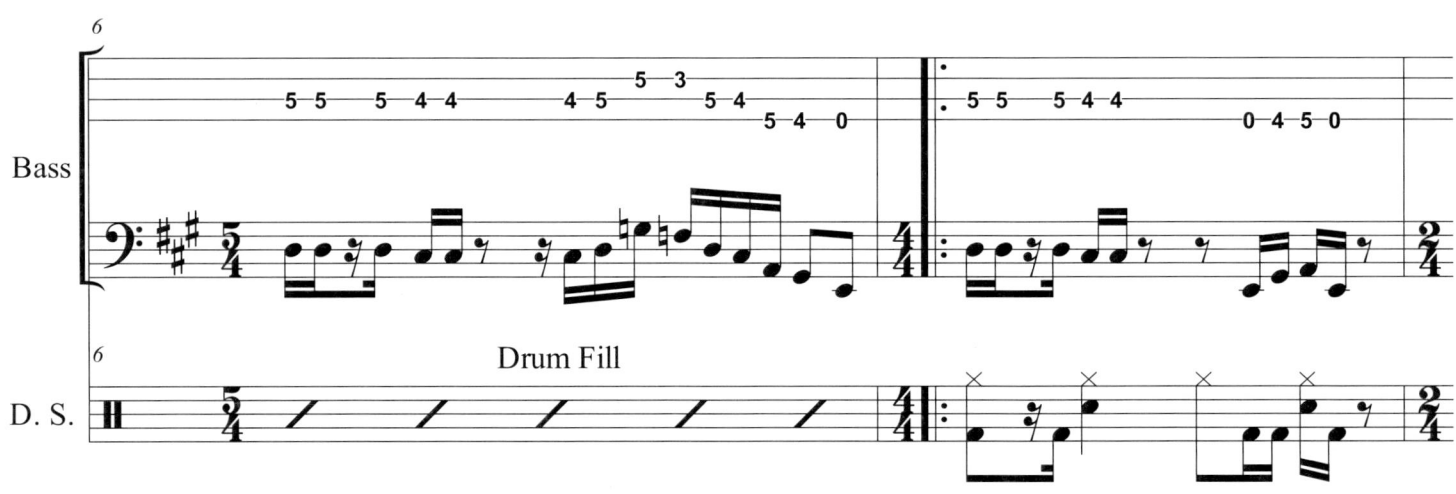

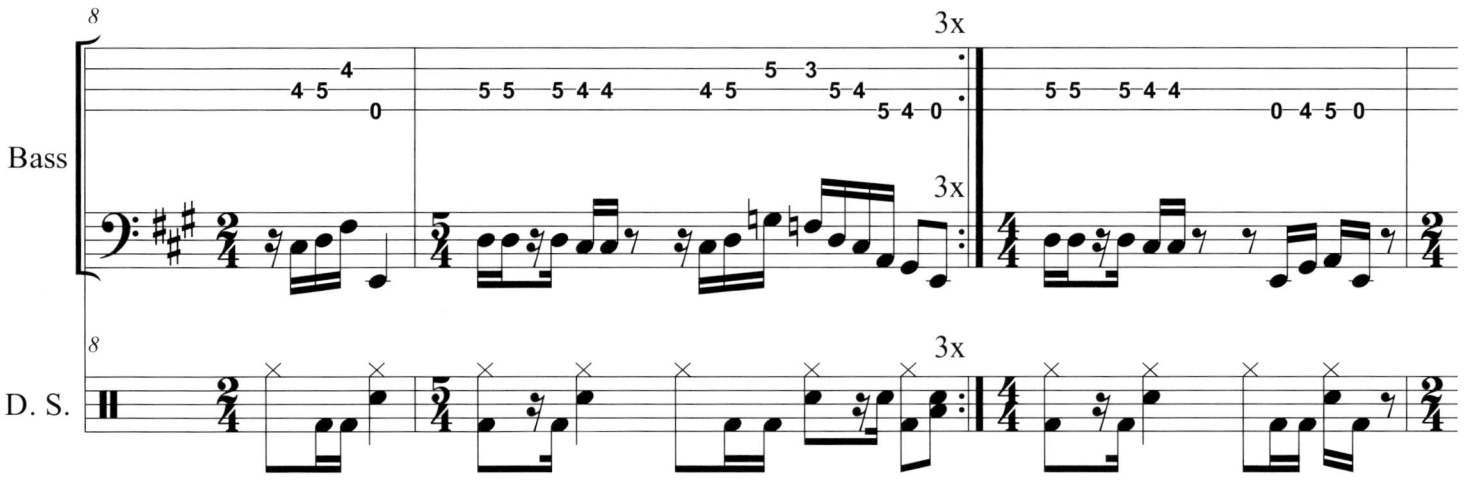
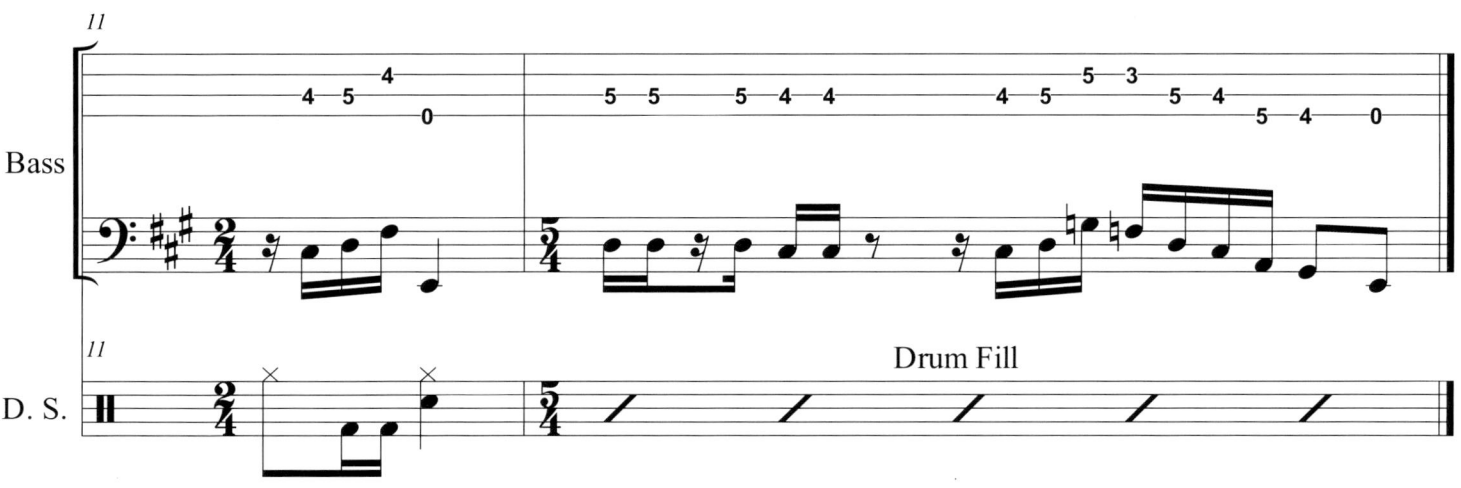

71

Rhythm 49

Example 49 features a bass solo. Now that you're at the end of the book take a ripping solo over the form. The drums will be playing along while on the cd the bassist will be playing accompany, so you're free to fill it up.

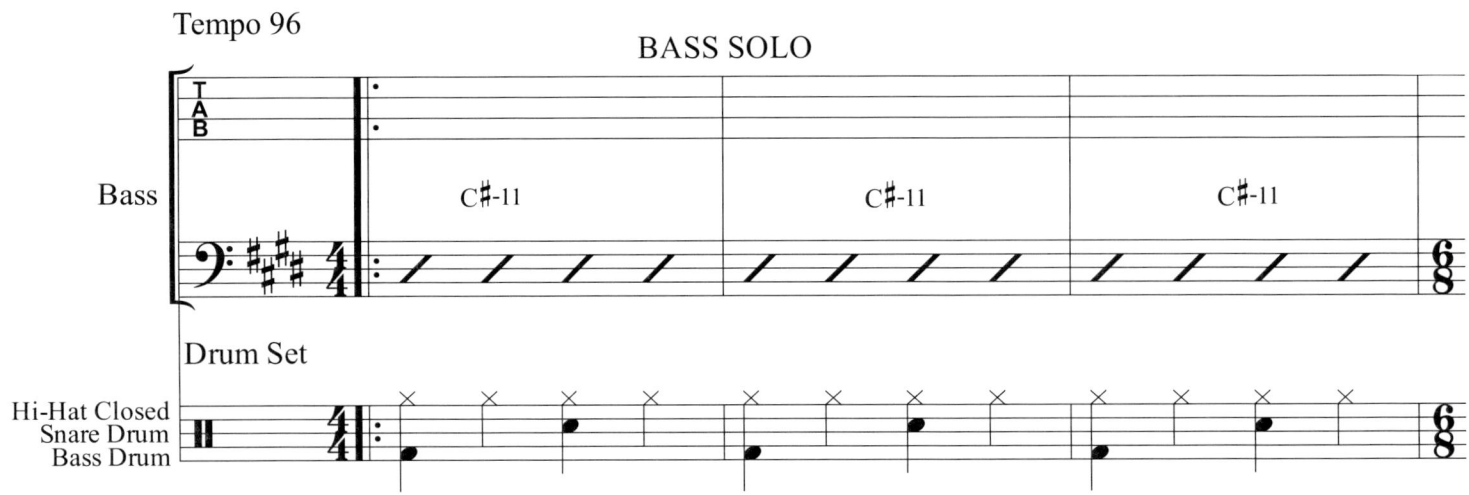

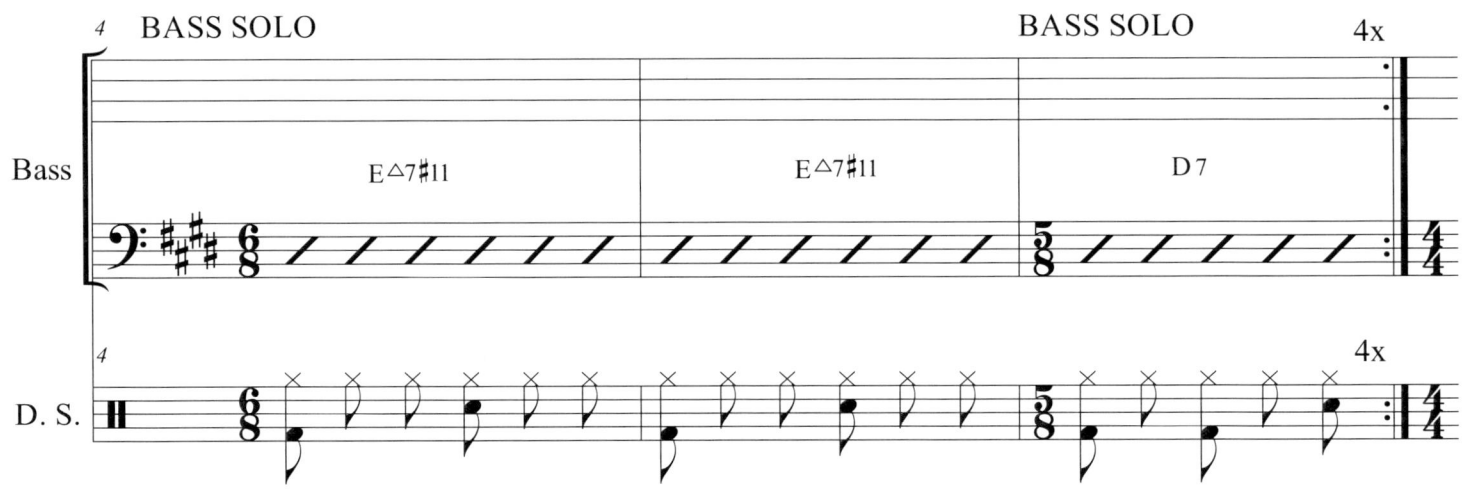

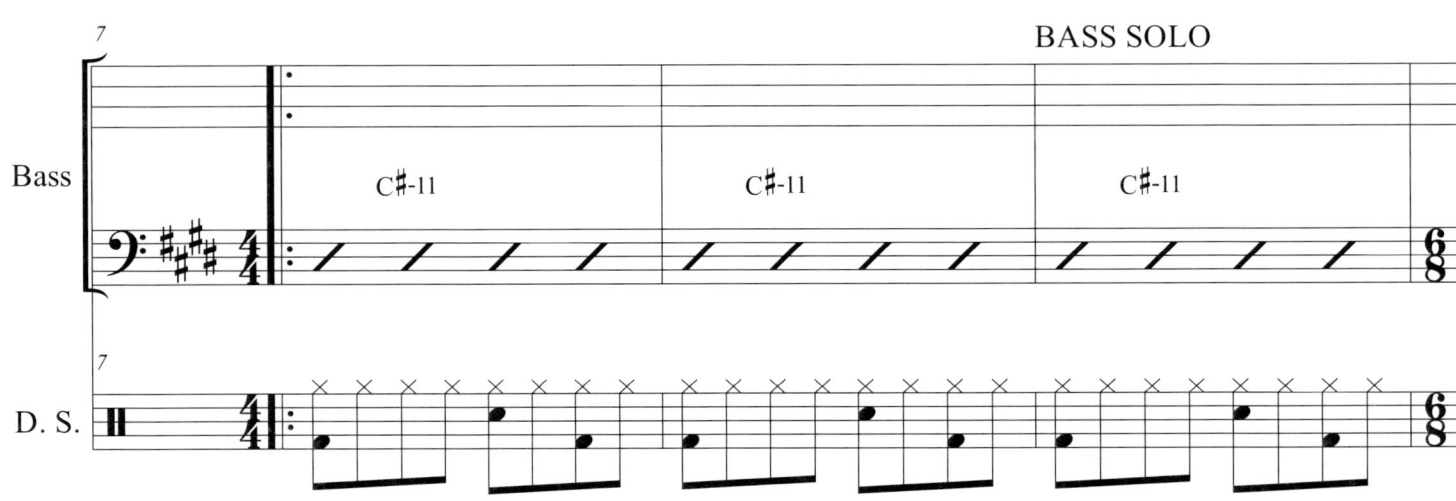

Rhythm 50

Lastly, this track is for the drummer to solo over. There are hits in the vamp for you to keep in mind as well as odd time bars. The bass will be playing the hits at first then a groove over the time. On the cd the drummer will be playing time so you are free to fill it up!

Tempo:180

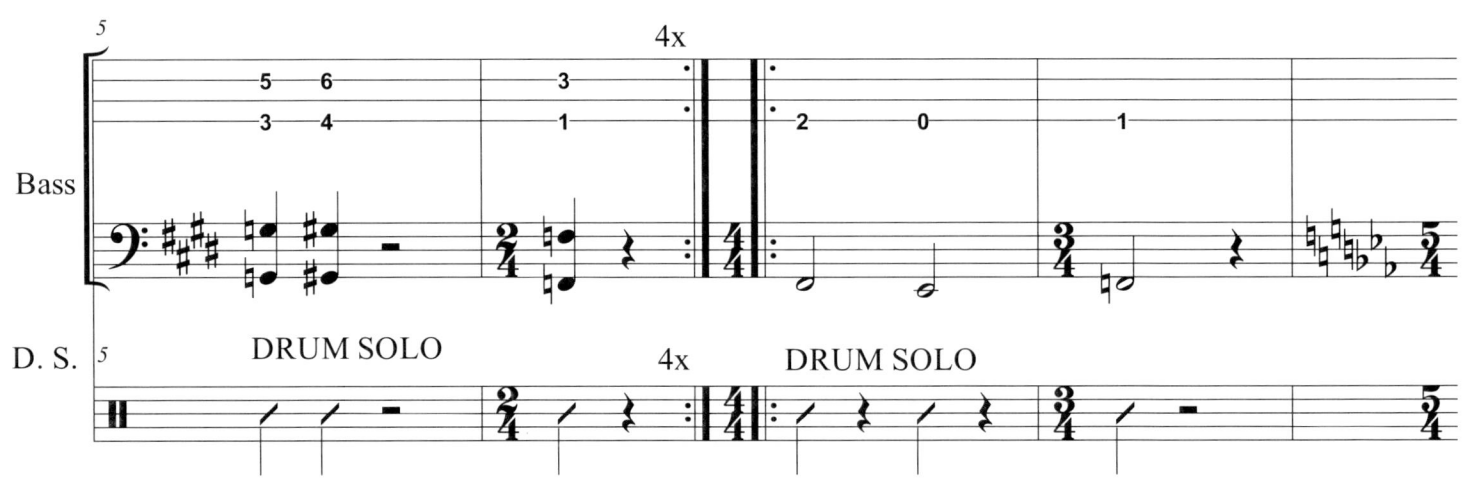

About the Author

Jason Prushko

Jason Prushko is an American musician originally from Shelton, CT now residing in Brooklyn, NY. He attended The New School for Jazz & Contemporary Music (New York, NY) where he received a Bachelor's degree in Music Performance. Fluent in many styles of music, Jason performs in many settings including freelance performing jobs, session/studio drumming and percussion, and has residency Jazz gigs in Brooklyn, NY as well as having upheld many through out CT. Jason is also a co-founder and co-composer for the American rock band *Mean Little Blanket* (www.meanlittleblanket.com). Jason is available for any style of studio/session drumming, live performances and private lessons for students of any skill level and any style of interest. www.jasonprushko.com

About the Author

Corey Dozier

Hailing from Texas, Corey Stephen Dozier grew up playing double bass and electric bass in jazz combos, orchestras and rock bands. He attended Houston's prestigious High School for the Performing and Visual Arts. On scholarship, he then went on to attend The New School for Jazz and Contemporary Music in New York City. At The New School he began playing and gigging with Jason Prushko, eventually founding the Brooklyn-based progressive rock band, Mean Little Blanket. Along with the band, the two friends also play numerous jazz, hip hop, and salsa gigs in the New York area. It is there they continue a never-ending search for new rhythms and harmonies to incorporate into their musical bag of tricks.